Rebuilding the United States

What I Would Do as President

DOUGLAS W. SABBAG

ISBN: 0983550662
ISBN-13: 978-0-9835506-6-2

Dedication

I dedicate this book and my Presidential Campaign to my wife: Evelyn, without whom neither of those efforts would have been accomplished nearly as well, or as professionally.

I also thank her for providing her complete and unwavering support throughout all of these steps, which so few may travel in their lives, but I was allowed to with her love, instead of anything less.

Table of Contents

DOUGLAS W. SABBAG

Table of Figures

DOUGLAS W. SABBAG

Prologue

Well, luckily you've somehow acquired this book, so you have in your hands the outline of how we can rebuild the United States of America. Please continue reading. I'm confident you'll agree this presents many common sense ideas which will greatly improve our country. And, I hope once you read these possibilities, you'll look forward to helping me make them happen.

Some people might suggest that America is doing fine and doesn't need to be rebuilt. But, there are too many statistics, graphics, general information, empirical observations and warning signs, which conflict with that belief. And, if nothing else, I doubt many would argue that there isn't plenty of room for improvement.

We've all heard the statistics of the decline of the American Middle Class and the associated rise of the income gap. We watched the recent efforts of the "Occupy Wall Street" movement. Many of us hoped something productive would result in spite of the lack of cohesive focus, but the movement fizzled without any lasting result. Generally, we felt they were touching on something truly wrong with America, but, like their effort, it all seemed too large and nebulous to directly confront, or solve.

The basis for this nebulous problem is directly related to the solution: our American Principles. Specifically, Justice for ALL, which is being fundamentally eroded and diminished by the successful efforts of Special Interest groups. The key to the success of these Special Interest groups is utilizing the *Achilles Heel of America*; money. This leverages our politicians away from the general good and toward their specific goals.

Whereas the diminishment of our American Principles is the problem, these Principles also represent the best and strongest solution. America's greatest strength and what set her apart from the rest of the world was the introduction and application of these Principles, as designed by our Founding Fathers. The ongoing evolution of these Principles via Constitutional Amendments, has maintained our society as a healthy growing democracy with all the associated benefits. These fundamental Principles of Right vs Wrong and Justice for All provide the road map for us to follow to refocus on the American Dream and set this ship of State on her proper course.

Please read on to see what I have in mind per our Principles and good old American common sense. We can rebuild our country for our mutual benefit, including the Special Interests, since what is best for us, the average citizens, is best for them too.

Chapter 1. Federal Sales Tax Instead of Income Tax

In order to fix something it's important to understand it. So let's review the history of the U.S. Federal Income Tax System.

Article I, Section 8, Clause 1 of the United States Constitution (the "Taxing and Spending Clause"), specifies Congress's power to impose "Taxes, Duties, Imposts and Excises", but Article I, Section 8 requires that, "Duties, Imposts and Excises shall be uniform throughout the United States."

In order to help pay for its war effort in the **American Civil War**, Congress imposed its first personal income tax in 1861. It was part of the **Revenue Act of 1861** (3% of all incomes over US $800). This would have resulted in the exemption of many citizens due to lower average income.

However, by 1862, the United States government realized that the war would not end quickly and that the revenue generated by this income tax couldn't be sufficient. As a result, before any income tax was collected under the first system, the Revenue Act of 1862 was passed in July of 1862. The act was signed into law by President Lincoln on July 1, 1862.

The Revenue Act of 1862 contained three main provisions, with the primary goal of increased revenue. The three provisions were:

> 1. *The creation of the office of the Commissioner of Internal Revenue, a department whose duty was to ensure the collection of taxes,*
> 2. *The levying of excise taxes on many every day goods and services, and*
> 3. *An adjustment to the income tax that was created under the Revenue Act of 1861.*

The Revenue Act of 1862, section 92, states that: "*duties on incomes herein imposed shall be due and payable*" *in 1863 and each year thereafter until and including 1866 "and no longer."*

In 1894, Democrats in Congress passed the **Wilson-Gorman tariff**, which imposed the first peacetime income tax. The rate was 2% on income over $4000, which meant fewer than 10% of households would pay this tax. The purpose of the income tax was to make up for revenue that would be lost by tariff reductions.

In 1895, the **United States Supreme Court**, in its ruling in *Pollock v. Farmers' Loan & Trust Co.,* found a tax based on receipts from the use of property to be unconstitutional. Due to the political difficulties of taxing individual wages without taxing income from property, a federal income tax was impractical from the time of the *Pollock* decision until the time of the ratification of the Sixteenth Amendment.

Congress proposed the Sixteenth Amendment (ratified by

the requisite number of states in 1913), which states:

> *The Congress shall have power to lay and collect taxes on incomes, from whatever source derived, without apportionment among the several States, and without regard to any census or enumeration.*

Therefore, in 1913, the 16th Amendment to the Constitution made the income tax a permanent fixture in the U.S. tax system. The amendment gave Congress legal authority to tax income and resulted in a revenue law that taxed incomes of both individuals and corporations.

In fiscal year 1918, annual internal revenue collections passed the billion dollar mark, rising to $5.4 billion by 1920. With the advent of World War II, employment increased, as did tax collections, to $7.3 billion. The *withholding tax* on wages was introduced in 1943 and was instrumental in increasing the number of taxpayers to 60 million and tax collections to $43 billion by 1945. Thus, the US Federal Income Tax was firmly in place and has remained in place.

But who's paying this tax? Mostly, the working citizens of America through withholding a portion of their earned income. From **Figure 1**, it might be noted that in 2011 there were approximately 136 million taxpayers, i.e., IRS Tax returns filed. However, the total population of the United States is closer to 318 million people. Remember this fact for a later discussion.

Corporations, which are also subject to Income Taxes, are assessed their tax liability per their annual profit, after expenses. Their *gross profit* is determined by the difference in their official bank account balance from December 31st of the prior year to December 31st of the current tax year, or whichever fiscal calendar they choose. Then their expenses and any other write-offs are subtracted from that amount, leaving their net / reportable profit from which their tax liability is calculated.

Table 1. Summary of Federal Income Tax Data, 2011

	Number of Returns*	AGI ($ millions)	Income Taxes Paid ($ millions)	Group's Share of Total AGI (IRS)	Group's Share of Income Taxes	Income Split Point	Average Tax Rate
All Taxpayers	136,585,712	8,317,188	1,042,571	100%	100.0%		
Top 1%	1,365,857	1,555,701	365,518	18.7%	35.1%	> $388,905	23.5%
1-5%	5,463,429	1,263,178	223,449	15.2%	21.4%		17.7%
Top 5%	6,829,286	2,818,879	588,967	33.9%	56.5%	> $167,728	20.9%
5-10%	6,829,285	956,099	122,696	11.5%	11.8%		12.8%
Top 10%	13,658,571	3,774,978	711,663	45.4%	68.3%	> $120,136	18.9%
10-25%	20,487,857	1,865,607	180,953	22.4%	17.4%		9.7%
Top 25%	34,146,428	5,640,585	892,616	67.8%	85.6%	> $70,492	15.8%
25-50%	34,146,428	1,716,042	119,844	20.6%	11.5%		7.0%
Top 50%	68,292,856	7,356,627	1,012,460	88.5%	97.1%	> $34,823	13.8%
Bottom 50%	68,292,856	960,561	30,109	11.55%	2.89%	< $34,823	3.13%

*Does not include dependent filers.

Figure 1 – Summary of Federal Income Tax Data, 2011

Then there are various special exemptions, tax subsidies and other unique tax advantages for Corporations which allow greatly reduced tax liabilities even for those with a declared profit.

Summary of five-year tax rates for 288 companies, 2008-2012

Effective tax rate group	# of cos.	% of cos.	2008-12 ($-billion)			Ave. 5-yr profit ($-mill.)	
			Profits	Tax	Ave. Rate	Pre-tax	After-tax
Less than 17.5%	119	41%	$929.6	$71.4	7.7%	$7,812	$7,212
17.5% to 30%	107	37%	1,001.6	246.8	24.6%	9,360	7,054
More than 30%	62	22%	401.2	134.6	33.6%	6,470	4,299
All 288 companies	288	100%	$2,332.4	$452.8	19.4%	$8,098	$6,526
93 Ultra-low tax companies							
Zero or less	26	9%	$169.5	$-8.7	-5.1%	$6,519	$6,853
Less than 10%	67	23%	465.0	7.0	1.5%	6,941	6,836

Courtesy of Citizens for Tax Justice

Figure 2 – Summary of Five Year Tax Rates for 288 Companies, 2008-2012

As seen from **Figure 2**, 41% or 119 of the 288 companies reviewed for this chart, paid less than a 17.5 % tax rate even though they collectively earned over $900 billion dollars. Worse yet, 9% or 26 of the 288 companies reviewed, paid either zero taxes, or actually received a tax refund while still declaring billions in profits (**Figure 3**).

Over the 2008-12 period seen in **Figure 2**, the 288 companies earned more than $2.3 trillion in pretax profits in the United States. Had all of those profits been reported to the IRS and taxed at the statutory 35 percent corporate tax rate, the 288 companies would have paid $816 billion in income taxes over the five years. Instead, the companies as a group were paid hundreds of billions of dollars in *tax subsidies*.

Tax subsidies for the 288 companies over the five years totaled a staggering $364 billion, including $56 billion in 2008, $70 billion in 2009, $80 billion in 2010, $87 billion in 2011, and $70 billion in 2012.

Almost half of the total tax-subsidy dollars over the five years — $173.7 billion — went to just 25 companies, each with more than $3.7 billion in tax subsidies.

26 Corporations Paying No Total Income Tax in 2008-12			
Company ($-millions)	08-12 Profit	08-12 Tax	08-12 Rate
Pepco Holdings	$ 1,743	$ −575	−33.0%
PG&E Corp.	7,035	−1,178	−16.7%
NiSource	2,473	−336	−13.6%
Wisconsin Energy	3,228	−436	−13.5%
General Electric	27,518	−3,054	−11.1%
CenterPoint Energy	4,078	−347	−8.5%
Integrys Energy Group	1,623	−133	−8.2%
Atmos Energy	1,486	−114	−7.7%
Tenet Healthcare	854	−51	−6.0%
American Electric Power	10,016	−577	−5.8%
Ryder System	1,073	−51	−4.7%
Con-way	587	−21	−3.5%
Duke Energy	9,026	−299	−3.3%
Priceline.com	557	−17	−3.0%
FirstEnergy	7,236	−216	−3.0%
Apache	7,580	−184	−2.4%
Interpublic Group	1,305	−28	−2.1%
Verizon Communications	30,203	−535	−1.8%
NextEra Energy	11,433	−178	−1.6%
Consolidated Edison	7,581	−87	−1.1%
CMS Energy	2,471	−26	−1.1%
Boeing	20,473	−202	−1.0%
Northeast Utilities	2,820	−19	−0.7%
Corning	3,438	−10	−0.3%
Paccar	1,711	−1	−0.1%
MetroPCS Communications	1,956	−1	−0.1%
TOTAL	$ 169,504	$ −8,676	−5.1%

Courtesy of Citizens for Tax Justice

Figure 3 – 26 Corporations Paying No Total Income Tax in 2008-12

Wells Fargo topped the list of corporate tax-subsidy recipients, with nearly $21.6 billion in tax subsidies over the five years. Other top tax subsidy recipients included AT&T

($19.2 billion), IBM ($13.2 billion), General Electric ($12.7 billion), Verizon ($11.1 billion), Exxon Mobil ($8.7 billion), and Boeing ($7.4 billion) (Figure 4).

25 Companies with the Largest TOTAL Tax Subsidies, 2008-12	
Company	2008-12 Tax Breaks
Wells Fargo	$ 21,574
AT&T	19,200
International Business Machines	13,223
General Electric	12,685
Verizon Communications	11,106
Exxon Mobil	8,673
Boeing	7,368
J.P. Morgan Chase & Co.	5,886
PNC Financial Services Group	5,343
Wal-Mart Stores	5,139
Procter & Gamble	4,986
Occidental Petroleum	4,880
ConocoPhillips	4,759
Chevron	4,486
Devon Energy	4,432
Exelon	4,211
NextEra Energy	4,180
Chesapeake Energy	4,102
Goldman Sachs Group	4,094
American Electric Power	4,083
Coca-Cola	4,046
Union Pacific	3,934
Intel	3,803
American Express	3,736
Southern	3,729
Total these 25 companies	$ 173,658

Courtesy of Citizens for Tax Justice; values are in billions

Figure 4 - 25 Companies with the Largest TOTAL Tax Subsidies, 2008-12

This is an obscene example of the power of lobbyists and money in the Halls of our government. This must end ASAP. Please vote for me – I will do the right thing and review these subsidies, just in case there is some valid logic behind this obscenity, then terminate all Federal Tax Subsidies to Corporations by working with Congress. Then Congress can blame the end of this gravy train on me, to their Corporate *constituents*.

But, enough about that depressing application of influence in our government, let's return to those who ARE paying taxes. For a broad view of who is paying the majority of the Income Taxes, examine **Figure 5**.

How the U.S. Government is Funded

% of total revenue

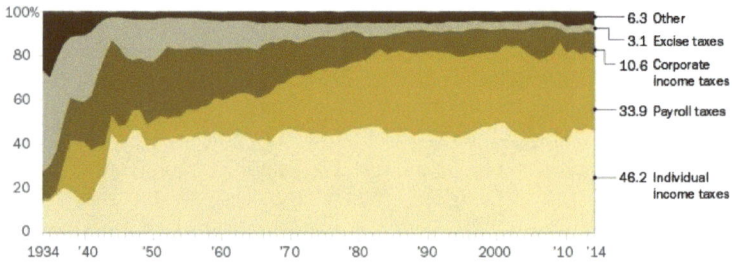

Source: Office of Management and Budget
PEW RESEARCH CENTER

Figure 5 - How the U.S. Government is Funded

From **Figure 5**, Individual and Payroll taxes comprise over 80% of the U.S. tax revenue, while Corporate Tax Revenue is closer to 10% of U.S. Tax Revenue. Therefore, W2 employees who are taxed before receiving their money pay the vast majority of our taxes, while those Corporations who pay any taxes at all, pay the least amount of the total paid.

Not surprisingly, this strikes me as quite unfair, verging on the immoral, and should be illegal. Perhaps you agree. This is an example of the conflict between *earned incomes* vs. *unearned incomes*, wherein the *earned* income is taxed first, and hardest. But, besides the philosophical unfairness of this conflict, this system is also very inefficient.

All year, every year, throughout their entire adult lives, hundreds of millions of Americans, including Corporations, are saving many if not all of their receipts from many if not all of their transactions, in computer systems, or, file folders, bags, shoe boxes, drawers, or God knows where.

After the New Year, most people will receive their W2s from their employers. Then they eventually have to sift through all of those saved receipts to categorize them and add up the categories.

Many of the millions of Americans filing their tax returns will choose to pay accountants / CPAs, or specialized tax return filing companies, or, do their tax returns themselves. Relatively recently, tax payers are able to utilize any of the various on-line systems, though many are still doing their tax returns manually, using pencils and paper.

Completing an Income Tax Return requires understanding which of the myriad of IRS rules, exemptions, and/or, algorithms each of the tax payers' receipts might fall under. Then after all of that, identifying which of the current tax tables this tax payer falls within to determine their tax liability balance.

Finally, these laborious and exacting efforts have produced their packet of 'filings', which must be specifically assembled and may then be mailed or electronically transmitted to the IRS by April 15th. With penalties and interest applied for late filings.

The IRS then employs an army of agents and accountants to review and re-process these millions of returns to determine *their analysis* of the tax balance for each of these millions of tax payers.

The net result of millions of these tax returns is that the citizen paid too much money to the government throughout the year, thus they are eligible for a tax refund. Since they paid too much money into their taxes all year long, this kept them from utilizing that portion of their own money. Additionally, these hard-working citizens receive no *interest* for their money being held by the government. The majority of people justify the conceptual cushion of these excess tax payments in the event the nebulous tax filing process results in them owing money.

For those who it is determined paid too little, a payment / collection effort is frequently the mandatory solution, which may easily require years to conclude. And in the worst cases, the IRS has powerful authorities to garnish wages, and/ or, seize any and all properties, funds, etc., except only the barest of essentials. Show any intent to purposely not pay your taxes and you are liable to spend years in jail. Many *tax criminals* are there right now.

All of this happens every single year, in America. Clearly, this is not an efficient, clean, or an easy process. I am sure we can do better than this.

And, there is another factor, which I pointed out earlier in this chapter. While there are currently approximately 318 million Americans, only 136 million were required to file IRS tax returns. So, basing our tax revenue on less than half of the total population is another one of the inefficient results of taxes based upon *earnings*.

Rather than taxing people and Corporations on their earnings, which is a very complicated, nebulous, inefficient, and even unfair process, I am suggesting taxing every entity, i.e., everyone including corporations, at the time that money is spent. This would make 'paying your taxes' an extremely easy, seamless process. When you buy something not exempted, you would also be satisfying your tax responsibility. No extra paperwork, no annual filings, no more deductions from your paycheck. Buy something and you are done.

This shifts our taxation system from an earnings based tax system to a consumption based tax system. This is called a **Federal Sales Tax**, not to be confused with the European VAT Tax.

> **Note:** *I am clearly not suggesting a VAT tax, since in the VAT System, the seller charges a **Value Added Tax** to the buyer, and the seller pays this VAT to the government. However, if the purchaser is not an end user, but the goods or services purchased are costs to its business, the tax it has paid for such purchases can be deducted from the tax it charges to its customers.*

That would not work in our case, since the resulting paperwork of the VAT System is not something I want to introduce to American businesses. One of the benefits of doing away with the current Income Tax System is to reduce the associated paperwork for everyone.

I would also suggest that there should be *Federal Sales Tax Exemptions* which would be applicable to all entities at time of purchase. These would be:

1. Food as defined by the Government's SNAP (Food Stamp) Program.

2. *Primary* (only for personal habitation) housing costs, i.e., mortgages / rent; including the standard utilities and insurance of their home.

3. Medical costs: equipment, services, drugs, anything related to the medical industry.

4. Education costs, i.e., tuition, uniforms, books, tutors.

5. Labor / employees / professional services.

6. Inheritance.

7. Court ordered judgments.

Considering the wide array of exemptions provided, the majority of standard purchases executed by financially challenged people would be tax free. Exemptions are the response to the common claim that a consumption tax is a *Regressive Tax*. This is generally defined as: "*A tax that takes a larger percentage from low-income people than from high-income people.*"

With a 10% Federal Sales Tax, the more anyone spends, including Corporations, the more they pay, with no cap, no limits. But, with the Federal Sales Tax Exemptions in place, peoples' primary expenditures would be tax free. This greatly diminishes the possibility of this being a Regressive Tax.

Granted, there would still be taxes on some standard purchases such as: clothing, entertainment, communication and automobile / transportation costs. But, the majority of these are either discretionary, and/ or, are infrequent purchases.

All other transactions of money in the United States of

America would therefore be taxed when purchased. This would include all goods and products, except fiduciary instruments such as securities, often referred to as *stocks*, which would only be taxed when sold, and then *only on the profit*.

This brings up the Capital Gains Tax. Currently, the United States has one of the highest Capital Gains tax rates in the world. As of 2015, our Capital Gains Tax Rate is the 6th highest in the world (Figure 6). However, that only displays our *Average* Capital Gains rate, as Americans we are also subject to the specific State Taxes applicable to us, determined by where we live.

As you can see in Figure 7, there are many States which will bring a taxpayers' total Capital Gains Tax liability up to a higher level than this average Capital Gains rate. This chart also happens to include the higher rates that are currently being proposed by President Obama. By relating the two charts, we can see that if you live in California, your total Capital Gains Tax liability is actually equal to the third highest in the world.

Table 2. Top Marginal Tax Rate on Capital Gains, by OECD Country, 2015

Rank	Country	Rate
1	Denmark	42.0%
2	France	34.4%
3	Finland	33.0%
3	Ireland	33.0%
5	Sweden	30.0%
6	United States	28.6%
7	Portugal	28.0%
7	United Kingdom	28.0%
9	Norway	27.0%
9	Spain	27.0%
11	Italy	26.0%

Figure 6 - Top Marginal Tax Rate on Capital Gains by OECD Country, 2015

Table 1. Top Marginal Tax Rate on Capital Gains, by U.S. States, 2015 and Under President Obama's Proposal

Rank	State	State Rate	Combined Rate	Rate Under Obama Budget
1	California	13.3%	33.0%	37.2%
2	New York*	8.8%	31.5%	35.7%
3	Oregon	9.9%	31.0%	35.2%
4	Minnesota	9.9%	30.9%	35.1%
5	New Jersey	9.0%	30.4%	34.6%
6	Vermont	9.0%	30.4%	34.6%
7	Maryland*	5.8%	30.3%	34.5%
8	Maine	8.0%	29.8%	34.0%
9	Iowa*	9.0%	29.6%	33.6%
10	Idaho	7.4%	29.4%	33.6%
11	Hawaii*	7.3%	29.4%	33.6%
12	Nebraska	6.8%	29.1%	33.3%
13	Connecticut	6.7%	29.0%	33.2%
14	Delaware	6.6%	29.0%	33.2%
15	West Virginia	6.5%	28.9%	33.1%

Figure 7 - Top Marginal Tax Rate on Capital Gains, by U.S. States, 2015 and Under President Obama's Proposal

By switching to the consumption tax system / Federal Sales Tax System, our Federal Capital Gains rate would plummet to 10%, and that would only occur / be paid, when you sell your security / stock. This distinction continues the inspiration already in place for people to buy stocks and avoid paying any taxes until they sell them. These taxes would only apply if they earned a profit.

Life Insurance / Annuities would be taxed when paid into, and/or when their respective premium is paid as would be the case with all other insurance policies, i.e., auto insurance, liability, errors and omissions, Workman's Compensation, etc.

How much tax revenue would this Sales Tax System provide? Well, the retail sales for 2014, excluding food sales, were $4.626 trillion. 10% of that would provide approximately **$500 billion**. But, as noted above, retail sales are not all that would be taxed.

The gross domestic product (GDP) of the United States for 2014 was $17.3 trillion. Just over 18% ($3 trillion of GDP) is from Government spending, which would not be taxed. That leaves $14 trillion, of which 10% would provide: **$1.4 trillion.**

Now considering my proposal to terminate Corporate Tax Subsidies, that nearly $100 billion per year, would no longer be deducted from our revenue. Thus adding another **$100 billion** into our annual budget.

Imports are not counted in GDP, but would be taxed by the new Sales Tax, when purchased. And if being imported from 3rd world nations, would also be subject to the new Trade Tariffs (Chapter 5). The 2013 amount of imports were $2.446 Trillion. Not counting the new Tariffs, just the Sales Taxes on imports would provide another **$250 billion**.

The approximate Federal Sales Tax income and the savings by ending the Corporate Subsidies would amount to over **$2.2 trillion** of tax revenue. Currently the IRS receives **$2.1 trillion** from Federal Income Taxes. So, without even counting all the other transactions, i.e., insurance, stocks, etc., which would also be taxed, the Federal Sales Tax System would efficiently and fairly **exceed** the current Federal Income Tax revenue stream and do it without the April 15th filing madness.

In addition, being a consumption tax system rather than an earnings tax system, any American entity which spends money would be paying taxes, as opposed to the current system wherein less than half of Americans are *taxpayers*. This would further distribute the tax liability across more entities thereby lessening each individual's load.

By the way, that $2.1 trillion income tax revenue is less than half of the total revenue of the US Government, which for 2014 was $5.75 trillion. Overall, I estimate that between the new Sales Tax System and the return to normal tariffs in our global trade (Chapter 5), our total US Tax Revenue would more than triple. Which does not include the increased spending which would result from both the end of Federal Income Tax wage deductions and the re-shoring of American Manufacturing.

There are many details necessary to codify and put this plan into action. For it to succeed, I would utilize the expertise and resources of the financial, governmental and legal experts of our country and/or the world, to work toward further refining the system specifics. The goal is to fairly and efficiently acquire the needed revenue for our country to function in a healthy manner. Whether 10% is the correct amount to tax could be much better determined given these additional expert inputs.

While 10% was chosen as a starting point, it does appear that this percentage would provide more tax revenue than we are currently receiving from the Income Tax System. Initially our tax revenue does need to be higher than what our straight operating costs are, in order to pay off our National Debt and refund the Social Security Trust Fund. Appropriate adjustments could be made as conditions change.

The current Federal Income Tax System is unfair, unwieldy and inefficient. We can clearly do much better. Given that the proposed Federal Sales Tax system will greatly exceed the current revenue coming in from the Income Tax System, in the next chapter I will describe how best to distribute, or spend, those additional trillions of dollars to even further improve the lives of Middle Class Americans.

Chapter 2. Sales Tax Revenue: Distribution Universal Health Care

The United States of America does not have a Universal Health Care System. But, these countries (and others), do:

- **Africa**: Rwanda, Algeria, Egypt, Ghana, Libya, Mauritius, Morocco, South Africa, and Tunisia.
- **Asia**: Bhutan, Bahrain, Brunei, China, Hong Kong, India, Iran, Israel, Japan, Jordan, Kazakhstan, Kuwait, Macau, Malaysia, Mongolia, North Korea, Oman, Pakistan, Qatar, Saudi Arabia, Singapore, South Korea, Sri Lanka, Syria, Taiwan, Tajikistan, Thailand, Turkey, Turkmenistan, and UAE.
- **Europe**: Albania, Austria, Andorra, Belarus, Belgium, Bosnia and Herzegovina, Bulgaria, Croatia, the Czech Republic, Denmark, Estonia, Finland, France, Georgia, Germany, Greece, Hungary, Iceland, Ireland, Italy, Latvia, Liechtenstein, Lithuania, Luxembourg, Malta, Moldova, Monaco, the Netherlands, Norway, Poland, Portugal, Romania,

Russia, San Marino, Serbia, Slovakia, Slovenia, Spain, Sweden, Switzerland, Ukraine,   and the United Kingdom.

- **North America**:   Barbados, Canada, Costa Rica, Cuba, Mexico, Panama, and Trinidad and Tobago.
- **South America**:   Argentina, Brazil, Chile, Colombia, Peru, Uruguay, and Venezuela.
- **Oceania**: Australia and New Zealand.

As an American, what does this list make you wonder? It inspires me to wonder what is wrong with the United States. Especially considering many of those countries have managed to provide Universal Health Care to all of their citizens, and frequently to their temporary guests, while nevertheless having only a fraction of the American GDP / economy! Call me crazy, but I firmly believe we can accomplish what those countries provide to their citizens; and we can do it even better!

Obviously the big questions are how much will it cost and how do we pay for it? Let's consider cost first.

As a general approximation of the cost, it is fairly well accepted that currently, $4000 - $5000 per person/year, should be the ball park cost. Given approximately three hundred and twenty million Americans, that adds up to approximately $1.3 – $1.6 trillion a year.

So how would we pay roughly one and a half trillion dollars a year? As displayed in Figure 8, we can see that currently we are already spending close to $500 billion on Medicare and almost $300 billion on Medicaid, plus $55 billion for Veterans Health.   That total of $855 billion is approximately $2,700 per capita, (per person / per year). However, a Universal Health Care System will include everyone, so this would effectively replace Medicare / Medicaid, VHA, etc., which would allow us to redirect that nearly $900 billion toward the new, Universal, system.

Besides the current government expense of $2,700 per capita, the citizens are making up the difference with insurance premiums and direct payments, bringing the current total per capita costs of medical care in America to roughly $8,500.

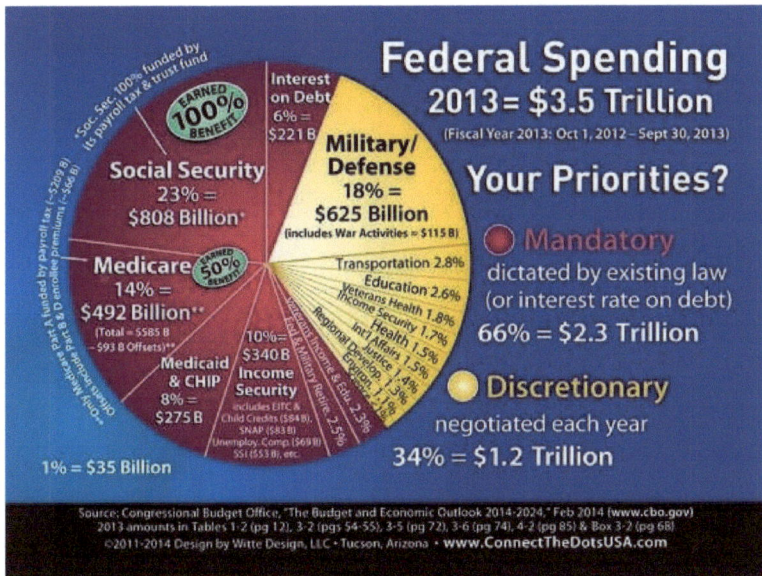

Figure 8 - Federal Spending

As a result, between government payments and personal payments, we're already spending roughly twice as much as the other developed nations on medical care. Something is drastically wrong. It's unacceptable that it should cost drastically more to provide medical services to Americans than it costs to provide the same level of care in other countries. Why would Italian, British, French or German people cost so much less than Americans to care for?

Is our quality of care so much better that it warrants spending at least twice as much for it?

A good approach to assess the quality of American medical services is the life expectancy of Americans as compared to the other countries' populations. Using this as a measuring stick, the clear answer is NO. The average life expectancy of an American ranks 36th out of the world, as shown in Figure 9.

Overall rank	Country	Overall life expectancy	Male life expectancy	Male rank	Female life expectancy	Female rank
1	Japan	84.6	85	1	87.3	2
2	Andorra	84.2	80.8	8	87.6	1
3	Singapore	84	82	2	87	3
4	Hong Kong	83.8	82	2	85.6	5
5	San Marino	83.5	82	2	85	11
6	Iceland	83.3	81.4	5	85.2	9
7	Italy	83.1	80.4	10	85.8	4
8	Sweden	83	81.4	5	84.6	13
9	Australia	83	80.5	9	85.5	6
10	Switzerland	82.8	80.4	10	85.4	7
11	Canada	82.5	80.4	10	84.6	13
12	Spain	82.5	79.5	15	85	11
13	New Zealand	82.1	80.2	19	84	19
14	Luxembourg	82	79.5	15	84.5	15
14	Israel	82	80	14	84	19
15	Norway	81.9	80.2	13	83.6	22
16	Austria	81.5	78.5	24	84.5	15
17	France	81.5	78	19	85	9
18	Netherlands	81.5	79.5	15	83.5	25
19	Ireland	81.4	79.2	22	83.6	22
20	Cyprus	81.2	79.1	23	84.3	18

Overall rank	Country	Overall life expectancy	Male life expectancy	Male rank	Female life expectancy	Female rank
21	Chile	81.2	80.1	38	82.3	33
22	Germany	81	78.5	24	83.5	25
23	Greece	81	78	28	84	19
24	Finland	81	78.0	28	84	19
25	South Korea	81	77.5	30	84.5	15
26	Malta	81	79.4	19	82.6	32
27	Belgium	81	78.5	24	83.5	25
28	United Kingdom	81	79.5	15	82.5	33
29	Liechtenstein	80.7	77.8	29	83.6	22
30	Taiwan	80.6	78	28	83.2	28
32	Lebanon	80.5	78.9	27	82.5	38
33	Portugal	80	76.9	37	82.8	31
34	Slovenia	80	77	35	83	30
35	Costa Rica	79.8	78.3	27	81.3	39
36	United States	79.8	77.4	32	82.2	35
37	Denmark	79.5	77	35	82	36
38	Cuba	79.4	77.4	32	81.4	38
39	United Arab Emirates	79.2	77.2	34	81.2	40
40	Brunei	79	77.5	30	80.5	46
41	Barbados	78.5	76.2	39	80.8	45
42	Kuwait	78.2	75.5	41	80.5	40
43	Czech Republic	78	75	42	81	42
44	Panama	77.8	74.6	44	81	42
45	Poland	77.5	73.5	51	81.5	37
46	Croatia	77.5	74.5	45	80.5	46
47	Dominica	77.5	75	41	80	52
48	Uruguay	77.3	74.2	48	80.4	49
49	Mexico	77.2	74.2	49	80.2	50
50	Maldives	77.2	76.2	39	78.2	73

Figure 9 - List by the World Health Organization (2014)

The list in Figure 9 shows that there are 35 countries

25

which have a longer life expectancy than Americans and most of those longer living populations have Universal Health Care for all of their citizens. We are all human beings who are clearly made of the same materials. We have the same structure and same organs. The logical conclusion is that we should cost roughly the same to maintain. Do our cars, homes, clothing, cell phones or other standard commodities cost drastically different amounts between us and the other developed countries? No, they do not. So, why does our medical care cost so much more?

Something is drastically wrong. Our government is already spending a vast amount of money, for only a limited number of citizens' medical care. Concurrently, our people are also personally spending another vast amount of money. Together we are spending easily twice as much as the next closest countries and well beyond that when compared to other, less developed countries. This is presented in Figure 10.

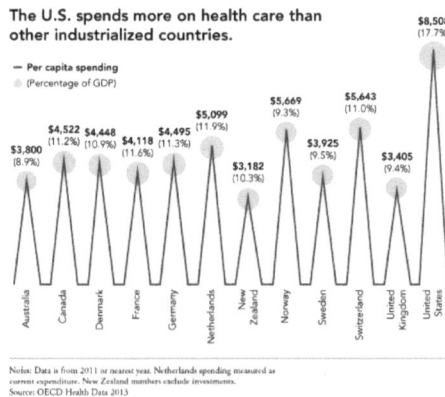

Figure 10 - The U.S. Spends More on Health Care than Other Industrialized Countries

Yet, for all this money being spent for medical care in America, there are 35 other countries enjoying a longer life expectancy. This indicates that those other countries' medical care systems are providing better care than we are, but for a lot less money.

Then again, it is well known that the health care system in America is exceptional, that our innovation is unprecedented, and that because of discoveries made in America, realistic hope for treatments against previously untreatable diseases is at an all-time high. Also, our medical training is the envy of the world, which inspires wealthy patients to fly here for their various high tech / high end medical procedures. How then, do we as a population, fail to rise to the top of the various health barometers?

As with many other features of our Capitalistic System, it has to be accepted that America has two levels of health care. Exceptional care for people with money and mediocre at best for those without. This widening disparity is surely dragging down our national averages and related numbers across the board.

Of course, there are also lifestyle and dietary differences between Americans and other populations, which have to be considered. America is well known as being the most obese nation on earth. I am sure that has huge (no pun intended), negative ramifications upon our national health averages.

Then, there is our corporate profit factor. To stay profitable, the large, for profit hospital chains, pharmaceutical corporations, insurance companies, and other medical associations divert health care resources to their shareholders, raising our health care costs, per capita.

It is also well documented that the administrative costs of American medical care are the highest in the world. Approximately 25% of our medical dollars are spent for the administration costs. There was a recent article that stated the Duke University Hospital has 900 hospital beds and 1300 billing clerks. Since we do not have a single payer system—defined as *"a system in which a single public or quasi-public agency organizes health care financing, but the delivery of care remains largely in private hands"*—a significant amount of effort is being expended figuring out how to bill the different insurers for their different services. In those countries with single payer systems, their administrative costs are generally in the 10% range with the top end reaching 15%.

Another disparity between American medical costs and other countries are the costs of drugs. Again, since we do not have a single payer system we're not able to negotiate those prices from the greatest leverage point with the various pharmaceutical corporations. As a result, America is spending much more than other countries for the same drugs and medical equipment.

Therefore, for all of those reasons, it makes a huge amount of sense to consolidate our health care system and provide all Americans with what is called *Universal Health Care*.

We are already spending at least twice, to as much as eight times more than other countries on a per person, per year basis, yet we're not living as long. We can do better than this. We *have* to do better than this. The Affordable Care Act (ACA) or *Obama Care* System was at least an effort toward this issue, but it still fell short of actually addressing these disparities and issues. And, because it did not institute a single payer system, it was not able to take advantage of the huge savings inherent to that system. The tremendous potential savings of having a single payer system might well cut our medical costs per capita in half.

As the other countries are experiencing, we should be able

to accomplish lowering our per capita costs from $8,500 to the $4,500 area, by realizing the tremendous savings in the administration costs, the costs of drugs and durable medical supplies, and the costs of the medical practitioners.

But, as was perhaps the limiting force when the ACA was being debated and designed, the interests of the various corporations involved in our medical industry must be taken into account. We do still want there to be an incentive for them to develop and provide new drugs and better techniques to keep the forward progress going. Given that a single payer system will provide huge negotiation power to greatly reduce their profits in America, we should concurrently *sweeten the pot*.

Keeping this in mind, as you might have noticed within the new *Federal Sales Tax System* design, there was an exemption for *medical costs*. This is not only to save the people from paying any taxes on medical expenses, like operations, drugs, etc., but also to allow the government to alleviate some of the expense of the medically focused corporations' financial transactions in developing and providing medically oriented products and services by not taxing them either.

Therefore, a pharmaceutical company would pay no taxes for their R & D costs, their chemicals, packaging, and distribution costs. A hospital would pay no taxes to buy their medical supplies. A medical professional association would pay no taxes on their stethoscopes, X-rays, MRI equipment, bandages, etc. Granted, non-technical / non-medically oriented commodities would still be taxed, for instance paper, desks, standard computers, etc.

As previously stated, the specifics of this would be finalized with the help of the various experts related to this area from around the nation. But, I'm confident that we can retain what is good about our medical industry by keeping a healthy financial profit in place, while concurrently drastically lowering our redundant costs and inefficiencies of the multiple payer system we are currently laboring under.

Finally, as the rough numbers indicate, we would be raising the U.S Governments' annual contribution toward healthcare from roughly $900 billion, up by as much as an additional $550 billion. But, as stated in the previous chapter, we'll have an entirely new taxation system which should provide more revenue than we are currently realizing from the Income Tax System. This additional revenue may be applied toward Universal Health Care.

All Americans would no longer have to pay any health insurance premiums. Besides no more Federal Income Tax deductions from our wages, we would also enjoy no more health insurance premiums to pay.

Still open for discussion, including calculations and careful consideration per the numbers, is whether or not we would still have to deduct the current Medicare / Medicaid amounts as we are from employees' wages. This was included in all calculations. The hope is that this, too, could eventually be ended. But the specific amounts available from the new Taxation System and the proposed re-instated tariffs need to be more thoroughly calculated, which is beyond my abilities while writing this book.

I look forward to utilizing the best minds in America, and/or the entire world, toward these mathematical estimations and determinations. The simple bottom line is that other countries are doing this; we can too. It's worth it to make sure we do it right, and I promise I will relentlessly endeavor to bring together the appropriate people and inspire them toward this goal.

Higher Education

Another area we need to address is training and education. Not that long ago, the cost of State and local Community Colleges was reasonable and many of our families could afford those costs for their children. But the negative pressures from the higher tuition and living costs along with the increased percentage of single parent households, with fewer resources available, are too much for too many people to handle. Rather than remaining in denial and not accepting the realities behind this societal change, to remain competitive and more importantly to provide our children with the tools they need to reach for the opportunities available, this must be resolved as a nation.

This downward spiral will only get worse as the manufacturing jobs which were the primary foundation of middle class America, continue to leave America. This topic will be addressed in Chapter 5 and Chapter 6. In the meantime, our younger generations of citizens are victims of a vicious cycle of not having the resources to pay for the extra training and higher education necessary to qualify for the reduced number of good jobs which predominately require training and higher education.

An outcome of this situation is that many of our young peoples' career options are limited to lower paying, less challenging jobs which leads to lowered self-esteem, a greater incidence of failed marriages, a general lowering of our consumer economic engine, and all the other ramifications therein. This will repeat itself through ensuing generations unless this cycle is broken.

In comparison, those who do manage to attend college,

whether they even finish or not, frequently have a large student loan / debt to pay off. This can take many years and, in some extreme cases, even their entire working lives to pay off. This debt is a great impediment to our young people, which hangs over them for many years. It further feeds into the negative cycle of not being able to afford to buy the training / education to qualify for the jobs to earn the money to enjoy the American Dream. Plus, a large number of *potential* doctors, lawyers, teachers, nurses, engineers, architects, artists, etc., are not advancing to their full potential because of these financial challenges and conflicts. They and our nation suffer every time this happens.

We can do better than this. We *must* do better than this. We have the infrastructure built, i.e., the schools, the teachers and the equipment to train people to be the best in the world. We can train people for careers in everything from plumbing to aerospace to graphic artists; anything and everything a young person can imagine and aspire to do, we have the facilities to get them there.

Another dynamic has been happening between the Community Colleges and our Federal Government over the last couple of decades. The Federal government has been providing greater resources for K – 12 schools which primarily service lower income neighborhoods, but in the Community Colleges arena, the Federal government has been doing the exact opposite. The majority of the governmental financial aid for higher education has been directed toward the elite universities. It has been speculated that this has been occurring because *their children* (of the government officials), don't attend Community Colleges anywhere nearly as much as they do higher echelon universities.

Students with the greatest needs who are entering the Community Colleges are less able to complete their programs, due in some part to not being able to afford the financial burdens during their matriculation. As a result, they leave these programs at a much greater rate without completing their programs. And, upon exit, they owe more than their counterparts in universities, whether they completed or not.

This must be turned around for our students in greatest need if we are to help rebuild the Middle Class in our country. My plan, as outlined further in this chapter, will address this inequity.

Another dynamic occurring in our American higher education colleges and universities are the foreign students who attend here. Currently, roughly 22 million people are enrolled in higher education studies in America. Of these, roughly one million are from foreign nations. The majority of these foreign students are from China and next are students from India. Of the Asian students, the majority are in what are called STEM (Science, Technology, Engineering and Mathematics) curriculum programs. These students are primarily enrolled in either engineering or computer science programs.

Many of the foreign students who graduate from STEM curriculum programs in America enter the American workforce through the H1B program. This program is designed to provide foreign workers to fulfill jobs in America *when Americans cannot be found to perform these tasks.* The exploitation and misuse of the H1B program is discussed in Chapter 6 However, for the purposes of this chapter, it may simply be noted that we do have a measurable deficiency in the number of Americans who are being properly educated / trained for the high tech / high paying jobs available in America. This is ludicrous and must end. ASAP.

This is not intended to suggest that there is any problem with foreign students in American schools. Instead, I am using their success to show that this is clearly the path we want to facilitate for American young people to travel. Whereas foreign students can matriculate in American schools and then fulfill American jobs because there are not enough trained Americans, this indicates that we have a serious problem.

Okay, so how much will this cost?

President Obama recently (Jan. 8, 2015), proposed this plan:

*President Obama said Thursday that he would propose a government program to make community college tuition-free for millions of students, an ambitious plan that would expand educational opportunities across the United States. The proposal would cover half-time and full-time students who maintain a 2.5 grade point average — about a C-plus — and who "make steady progress toward completing a program," White House officials said. It would apply to colleges that offered credit toward a four-year degree or occupational-training programs that award degrees in high-demand fields. The federal government would cover three-quarters of the average cost of community college for those students, and states that choose to participate would cover the remainder. If all states participate, the administration estimates, the program could cover as many as **nine million students**, saving them each an average of **$3,800** a year.*

Using President Obama's proposed plan numbers, nine

million students at $3,800 per year would equate to approximately $34 billion dollars.

Some background information: Currently, about 7.7 million Americans attend community colleges for credit, of which 3.1 million attend full time, according to the American Association of Community Colleges, relying on 2012 data. Overall, the federal government provides about $9.1 billion to community colleges; tuition from students provides $16.7 billion a year.

It would appear that Obamas' proposed plan has built in some room for growth from the current 7.7 million students to 9 million. That is realistic, since there should be an appreciable increase in students, given Government Subsidized Tuition.

This proposal should be amended to utilize the next wave of education: an internet / on-line education model. This method allows even greater numbers of students to access training / education programs without needing chairs, desks, classrooms, heating etc., and also allows them to access their selected courses on their own schedules. All at greatly reduced costs. Utilizing an on-line educational system should mean that the actual amount which the Federal Government would have to contribute would be somewhere between our current $9 billion in expenditures and the $34 billion Obama estimated.

Considering the myriad of details needed to put this plan into action, I would utilize the expertise and resources of the educational, application system programming, governmental and legal experts of our country to design and implement an on-line educational system so as to fairly and efficiently manage the staffing, computer system(s), and testing procedures, and manage their financial costs. The resulting program would provide the materials on-line, teacher support, and certification for each student who completes the courses.

We can do this.

Chapter 3. All Recreational Drugs Legalized

Currently, over 50 percent of inmates in federal prisons are there for drug offenses, according to an infographic recently released by the Federal Bureau of Prisons (Figure 11). That percentage has risen fairly consistently over the decades, beginning with 16 percent in 1970.

As the number of people convicted of drug offenses has gone up, the federal prison population has increased -- almost 790 percent since 1980, when there were only about 25,000 inmates, according to a 2012 Congressional Research Service report. Today, there are more than 215,000 inmates in federal prisons, the BOP reports. The per capita cost of each prisoner is $31,307. This totals almost $7 Billion dollars, per year. And that is just a small part of the total estimated costs of the *War on Drugs* which is over $41 Billion, annually.

Our 'War on Drugs', has aimed to eradicate drug abuse through strict laws and harsh enforcement within and beyond U.S. borders. The policies date back a century, though the term was only coined in 1971. And for many years, based upon the stated goals of this war, it has been a total failure.

U.S. Prison Population As Of Jan. 25, 2014

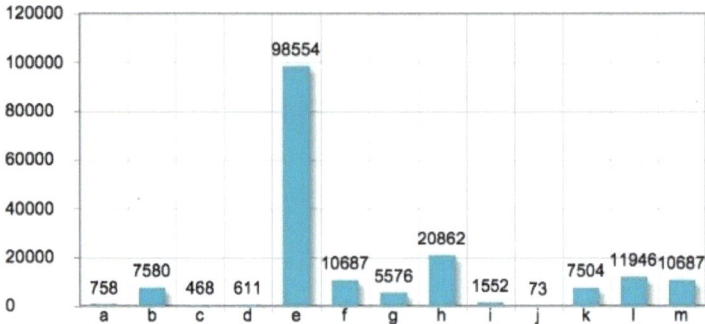

Chart Label	Offense	# of Inmates	% of Inmates
a	Banking and Insurance, Counterfeit, Embezzlement	758	0.4%
b	Burglary, Larceny, Property Offenses	7,580	3.9%
c	Continuing Criminal Enterprise	468	0.2%
d	Courts or Corrections	611	0.3
e	Drug Offenses	98,554	50.1%
f	Extortion, Fraud, Bribery	10,687	5.4%
g	Homicide, Aggravated Assault, and Kidnapping Offenses	5,576	2.8%
h	Immigration	20,862	10.6%
i	Miscellaneous	1,552	0.8%
j	National Security	73	0.0%
k	Robbery	7,504	3.8%
l	Sex Offenses	11,946	6.1%
m	Weapons; Explosives, Arson	10,687	5.4

Data is limited due to the availability of offense-specific information.

Figure 11 – U.S. Prison Population as of Jan. 25, 2014

Illicit drug use in America not been eradicated, it has been increasing. In 2012, an estimated 23.9 million Americans aged 12 or older, which is 9.2 percent of the population, had used an illicit drug in the past month. This is up from 8.3 percent in 2002. But when and why did the consumption of these drugs become illegal?

Prior to 1914, drug use on a Federal level in the United States was not regulated. However, there were local laws as early as 1860. In the 1890s the Sears & Roebuck catalogue, offered a syringe and a small amount of cocaine for $1.50. After this, the *Harrison Narcotics Tax Act of 1914* was a Federal Law which regulated and taxed the production, importation, and distribution of opiates and coca products.

> *"An Act To provide for the registration of, with collectors of internal revenue, and to impose a special tax on all persons who produce, import, manufacture, compound, deal in, dispense, sell, distribute, or give away opium or coca leaves, their salts, derivatives, or preparations, and for other purposes."*

The drafters of this law played on fears of *"drug-crazed, sex-mad negroes"* and made references to Negroes under the influence of drugs murdering whites, degenerate Mexicans smoking marijuana, and Chinamen seducing white women with drugs. Dr. Hamilton Wright testified at a hearing for the Harrison Act. Wright alleged that drugs made blacks uncontrollable, gave them superhuman powers and caused them to rebel against white authority. Dr. Christopher Koch of the State Pharmacy Board of Pennsylvania testified that *"Most of the attacks upon the white women of the South are the direct result of a cocaine-crazed Negro brain"*.

Before the Act was passed, on February 8, 1914, The New York Times published an article entitled *"Negro Cocaine 'Fiends' Are New Southern Menace: Murder and Insanity Increasing Among Lower-Class Blacks"* by Edward Huntington Williams, which reported that Southern sheriffs had increased the caliber of their weapons from .32 to .38 to bring down Negroes under the effect of cocaine. Despite the extreme racialization of the issue that took place in the buildup to the Act's passage, contemporary research on the subject indicated that black Americans were in fact using cocaine and opium at much lower rates than white Americans.

Recognizing that it was unconstitutional for the US government to simply outlaw drug sales and use, they employed a tactic that had been growing in popularity: They called it a tax. Instead of outlawing the drug trade, they required that anybody involved in it had to be registered and pay a tax. However, the tax was not equally applied; doctors and pharmacists were required to pay only a registration fee, while other people were required to pay a prohibitive tax on every sale. As a result, the sale of opiates and cocaine was effectively restricted to medical professionals "*in the course of their professional practice only.*" Others, unwilling or unable to pay the tax, would be charged with tax evasion and fined and/or imprisoned if they sold the restricted drugs. Thus, the federal government justified its actions as being constitutional because it was "*just using its power to tax.*"

The courts interpreted this to mean that physicians could prescribe narcotics to patients in the course of normal treatment, but not for the treatment of addiction. Although technically illegal for purposes of private distribution and use, the distribution, sale and use of cocaine was still legal for *registered* companies and individuals.

A 1918 commission called for tougher law enforcement, while newspapers continued publishing sensational articles about addiction related crimes. Congress responded by toughening up the Harrison Act; whereas the importation of heroin for any purpose was banned in 1924. After other associated laws were codified and enforced, the Uniform State Narcotic Act in 1932 is one example, the number of addicts of opium started to decrease to a level that in 1945 was about one tenth of the level in 1914.

Early in the 20th century, the United States—grappling with its first drug epidemic—gradually instituted effective restrictions; at home through domestic law enforcement and overseas by spearheading a world movement to limit opium and coca crops. By World War II, American drug use had become so rare, it was seen as a marginal social problem. The first epidemic was forgotten. However, the act of 1914 also marks the beginning of the modern, criminal drug addict and the American black market for drugs.

Fast forward to the 1960s, and drugs like marijuana, amphetamines, and psychedelics came on the scene as a new generation embraced drugs. With the drug culture exploding, our government developed new laws and agencies to address the problem. In 1973, the U.S. Drug Enforcement Administration(DEA) was created to enforce federal drug laws. In the 1970s, cocaine reappeared. Then, a decade later, crack appeared, spreading addiction and violence at epidemic levels.

Today, the DEA's biggest challenge is the dramatic change in organized crime. The drug use challenges which were successfully dealt with in the early 20th century were no longer as easily contained. While American criminals once controlled drug trafficking on U.S. soil, today sophisticated and powerful criminal groups headquartered in foreign countries control the drug trade in the United States. This business is driven by a demand for *recreational* drugs, which has created a multi-billion dollar industry. This industry is entirely *under the table*, i.e., not taxed, regulated, nor controlled in any manner. And that demand, for the most part, is not going down (Figure 12).

Table ES.1: Chronic Users of Cocaine, Heroin and Methamphetamine (Thousands)

	2000	2001	2002	2003	2004	2005	2006
Cocaine	2,578	2,661	2,634	2,812	2,823	2,775	2,777
Heroin	961	939	975	946	900	844	841
Methamphetamine	823	850	887	1,017	1,165	1,272	1,334
Marijuana	10,200	10,200	12,800	12,700	12,400	12,800	13,000

http://www.whitehouse.gov/ondcp

Figure 12 – Chronic Users of Cocaine, Heroin, Methamphetamine and Marijuana (Thousands)

The approximate amount of money being spent in America on these drugs is quite serious too (Figure 13), and it's all entirely underground. It's supporting the activities of the entities who are experts at avoiding governmental detection and it should be assumed their chosen focus and use of these funds is clearly not in the best interests of society, on any level. There are many indications that much of these funds are being diverted into supporting violence and even terrorism.

Table ES.3: Total Expenditures on Cocaine, Heroin, Methamphetamine and Marijuana ($ Billions)

	2000	2001	2002	2003	2004	2005	2006
Cocaine	$34.6	$35.0	$35.9	$40.1	$37.2	$37.9	$37.8
Heroin	$11.9	$12.3	$12.7	$12.1	$11.5	$10.8	$11.0
Methamphetamine	$11.7	$11.6	$12.5	$13.4	$15.7	$17.4	$17.9
Marijuana	$25.2	$25.2	$35.7	$36.9	$30.3	$33.5	$33.7
Total	$83.40	$84.10	$96.80	$102.50	$94.70	$99.60	$100.40

http://www.whitehouse.gov/ondcp

Figure 13 – Total Expenditures on Cocaine, Heroin, Methamphetamine and Marijuana ($Billions)

As of 2006, we can see that approximately $100 billion are funneled through this underground industry, annually. All indications point to this number increasing. From this, we must accept the reality that we are not winning the War on Drugs and, that as long as the funds from that lucrative industry remain underground, our society is being injured. Therefore, we have to address this. I propose that we change our efforts to those which we can and must win.

It is very clear that we are not going to succeed in ending the demand. And after spending extensive resources, in both money and casualties, over a period of many years toward ending the supply, globally and locally, **it is very clear we are not going to succeed in ending the supply either.** It should also be accepted that incarcerating hundreds of thousands of drug addicts only too frequently further ruins these peoples' lives, as opposed to the rare instance when it has actually rehabilitated them.

Therefore, I see only one way to accomplish our most rational goals for society as a whole, both cleanly and completely. We should terminate the basis of this underground industry by the full legalization of these drugs.

If the production and delivery systems were made legal, then we could regulate the quality to provide potentially dangerous drugs in as safe a form as possible for consumption. This would reduce the chances of medical emergencies from inappropriate ingredients and overdoses from varying and unpredictable strengths. The legal distribution of these products would also allow their taxation, which has already been enjoyed by those states that have enacted legalization laws for marijuana. Some of the income from the taxation could be earmarked for a national program of drug rehabilitation on an as needed basis. This is in direct contrast to the current financing of last resort drug rehabilitation for emergency situations.

Additionally, if drug use were no longer illegal, the anxiety of entering a drug rehabilitation program due to the legal and job related ramifications would be greatly reduced. This reality should not be overlooked as a great advantage of legalization for the benefit of the people who should be receiving help instead of either incarceration or the other stigmas which currently keep them alone in their plight.

And finally, the current illegal producers and distributors of these drugs would effectively be rendered pointless and out of business. There would be little value in dealing with them when you can just go to the store and buy higher quality products – legally. **This is the only way to put the illegal drug dealers out of business. This is the best way to win the 'War on Drugs'**.

With this proposal comes the fear that drug use would dramatically rise. Examining results from other municipal / State legalization programs reveals that this is an unreasonable concern.

> *"Health experts in Portugal said that Portugal's decision 10 years ago to decriminalize drug use and treat addicts rather than punishing them is an experiment that has worked."*
>
> *"There is no doubt that the phenomenon of addiction is in decline in Portugal," said Joao Goulao, President of the Institute of Drugs and Drugs Addiction, a press conference to mark the 10th anniversary of the law."*
>
> *"The number of addicts considered "problematic" — those who repeatedly use "hard" drugs and intravenous users — had fallen by half since the early 1990s, when the figure was estimated at around 100,000 people", Goulao said.*
>
> *"Other factors had also played their part however", Goulao, a medical doctor added.*
>
> *"This development can not only be attributed to decriminalization but to a confluence of treatment and risk reduction policies."*

And finally, considering that I am running as a Republican, it should be noted that the pure form of Republicans' beliefs are that each person is responsible for his or her own place in society. Government should enable each person the ability to secure the benefits of society for themselves, their families and for those who are unable to care for themselves. But, the Government is not responsible to guarantee success, only the opportunity. The core Republican philosophy is based on limiting the intervention of government into the individual's life. Government should only intervene in specific cases where society cannot effectively act at the individual level. The core belief is that individual destiny should be in the individual's hands.

With that in mind, it's my belief that it's not the business of the government to legislate a person's choice to use drugs. Perhaps that is best done by parents, in that they should raise their children to know better than to damage their bodies and minds by the use of recreational drugs.

However, once these children become adults, whether they choose to ingest alcohol, which is legal yet highly addictive and destructive on many levels, or tobacco which is at least as addictive and damaging, while also being legal, or, if they choose from the list of currently illegal drugs, the government should not attempt to legislate this choice. Note that this is not an attempt to suggest that any of these substances are good for us, but from alcohol and tobacco to marijuana and even heroin, the right to choose any of these should be left up to the individual; not by our Government.

I must also add that when a person leaves the privacy of their own home or any secure / private location, and enters a public space, especially when responsible for operating a vehicle, then the government does have the right to legislate and restrict the usage of any drugs which would render the person a danger to society. We already have laws and enforcement methods in place to address whenever a person becomes a danger to society while under the influence of any drugs. Of course, I would continue to support those very important laws.

Overall, our societies' best interests can clearly be best met in a responsible manner if we control and manage this drug industry, legally. Leaving it underground does not help us. **Only by controlling it can we declare that we have finally won the war on drugs.**

Chapter 4. Infrastructure Rebuild

During the Great Depression of the late 1930s, several programs were initiated to put unemployed people to work while also completing a vast array of municipal, state, and federal projects. These projects included: roads, bridges, airports, large electricity generating dams, hospitals, fire stations, stadiums, playgrounds, auditoriums, schools, theatres, gardens, libraries, courthouses, museums, sidewalks, post offices, swimming pools, community centers, zoos, tennis courts, and many others. Some even ranged outside of pure construction efforts into areas as diverse as art project, music, historical records, writing and reforestation. These programs were the Public Works Administration (PWA), the Works Progress Administration (WPA) and the Civilian Conservation Corps (CCC). As an aside, the CCC was the most popular of the New Deal Programs because of a combination of benefits to the participants and an increased awareness of nature and conservation by society as a whole.

The PWA was primarily focused on large scale public works projects wherein the government gave contracts to existing private construction companies. This group specifically functioned by making allotments to the various federal agencies; making loans and grants to state and other public bodies; and making loans without grants to the railroads. For example it provided funds for the Indian Division of the CCC to build roads, bridges and other public works on and near Indian reservations. The PWA had an initial two-year budget of $3.3 billion (compared to the entire GDP of $60 billion), and was the driving force of America's biggest construction effort up to that date. In total the PWA spent over $6 billion.

The WPA focused primarily on smaller projects and hired unemployed unskilled workers. This was a national program that operated its own projects in cooperation with state and local governments, which provided 10–30% of the costs. Usually the local sponsor provided land and often trucks and supplies, with the WPA responsible for wages. The WPA's initial appropriation in 1935 was for $4.9 billion (about 6.7 percent of the 1935 GDP), and in total it spent $13.4 billion.

The CCC focused specifically on providing young men with employment. An average worker in the CCC was a male between the ages of 18-23, who received a monthly salary of $30 ($480 in today's wages). $25 of that salary had to be sent home to his family. The participants implemented a national conservation program, which included flood control districts, reforestation and building parkways in remote areas. Over its 9 year existence, the entire budget was $3 billion; equivalent to $6 billion / year in current dollars.

The output of these programs created a large amount of the existing infrastructure we are still enjoying today. Which, it should be noted, has been well over 70 years.

Fast forward to today.

During a recent interview, U.S. Secretary of Transportation Anthony Foxx noted that the nation's transportation system is *"in a huge ditch."* In the same time frame, the U.S. Department of Transportation (USDOT) re-announced the solution in the form of the *GROW America* proposal. 'Re-announced' because that was the same title as the federal *surface transportation program* announced by the Obama Administration the previous year. But this time the Administration has identified a specific funding source: *taxing overseas corporate profits*, to pay for the estimated $478 billion, six-year program. Highlights of the GROW America proposal are:

- Increase the nation's overall investment in transportation by 45%, with a 29% increase in highway spending and a 76% increase in transit spending.
- $18 billion for a multi-modal freight program that strengthens America's exports and trade.
- $28.6 billion for passenger rail programs.
- Double funding for the Transportation Investment Generating Economic Recovery (TIGER) competitive discretionary grant program and create a new $6 billion highway and transit competitive grant program.
- Double the Transportation Infrastructure Finance and Innovation Act (TIFIA) program, which encourages utilization of innovative financing mechanisms.

This proposal's biggest challenge is the funding.

Currently, funding for the DOT is based upon the taxes of 18.4 cents per gallon of gasoline and 24.4 cents for diesel, which has been the same rate since 1993. Considering inflation since that time, the average federal highway dollar has lost over a third of its purchasing power. From Figure 14 it can be seen that the annual fuel tax income has dropped since 2007 by roughly $2 billion.

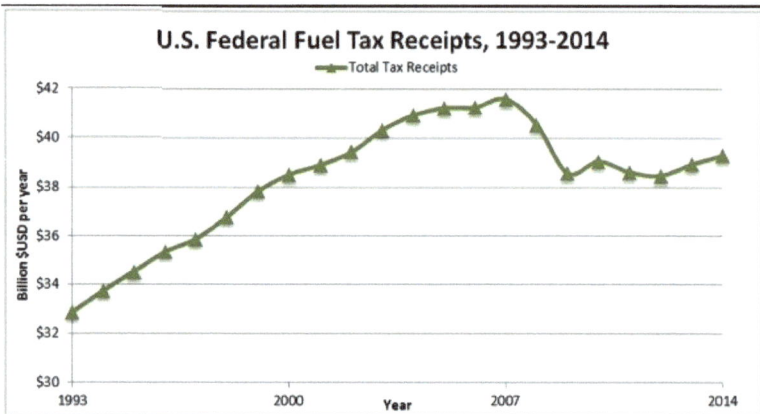

Figure 14 – U.S. Federal Fuel Tax Receipts, 1993-2014

It's difficult to predict if President Obama will accomplish moving the Grow America program forward by taxing overseas corporate profits, but if we don't address the deteriorating conditions of our nation's bridges and highways, we'll be picking up the pieces of many catastrophes, as they slowly but surely occur nationally.

11.5 percent, or 67,000 of the nation's 605,000 bridges, which the public statistics indicate are crossed by an average of 282,672,680 vehicles daily, were graded as "structurally deficient" by the Federal Highway Administration (FHWA). Bridges rated "structurally deficient" are in need of substantial repair or replacement, according to official inspections. Nearly 8,000 are both structurally deficient and "fracture critical", meaning they are designed with no redundancy in their key structural components, so that if one component fails the bridge could collapse.

The Federal Highway Administration estimates that the backlog of troubled bridges would cost $76 billion to eliminate. Meanwhile, the need is rapidly growing. Age is a major factor in bridge conditions. While most bridges are designed to last 50 years before a major overhaul or replacement, American bridges average 43 years old. Roughly half of the structurally deficient bridges are 65 or older. Today there are nearly 107,000 bridges 65 or older, and in just 10 years, one in four will be over 65.

Congress has repeatedly declared the condition and safety of our bridges to be of national significance. However, the money to fix them is getting harder to come by with declining fuel tax revenues. At the same time, Congress made the prospects for bridges even more unlikely by eliminating a dedicated fund for them in its latest update of the federal transportation program. The new law also reduces access to funds for 90% of structurally deficient bridges, most of which are owned by cash-strapped local governments.

As a country, we cannot allow this situation to continue unaddressed. This is clearly dangerous to the point of being deadly. We have to act as responsible stewards of our roads and bridges, regardless of any political agendas. I will personally work relentlessly with Congress once we have the new Federal Sales Tax in place to direct the necessary funds to address this issue. The Federal Highway Administration estimates it will cost $76 billion to eliminate these troubled bridges, so we simply have to bite the bullet and properly establish the budget to do this.

While we're catching up on our deteriorating bridges, we should also address our poorly constructed highways. They were built in a big rush in the 1950s for a much lower amount of wear and tear due to the assumption that the railroads would continue to carry the majority of the commodities of our nation. It's obvious that this is not what happened, yet the construction design did not change. Our roads do not reflect our construction abilities.

In Germany, they have what are frequently called the best roads in the world. These roads are built using freeze resistant concrete and a bituminous surface, and the roadbed and surface depth are supposedly greatly superior to American road thickness. I believe we can learn from the Germans and will seriously support doing so.

As the President, I will budget for the highway repairs to be done following better standards. Perhaps it would make sense to use the German standards / designs, but, not being a construction expert I will enlist their aid and utilize their knowledge and experience toward understanding how best to build highways so that they last longer and provide safer traction then what we currently produce. This approach must be applied to repairing our current highways instead of just repeating the low quality standards of today.

Another area we cannot allow to further deteriorate is our National Parks. Starting with the memorials and monuments in the Washington D.C. area, we have for too long barely maintained them and allowed them to deteriorate to the point that we are being reactive rather than proactively maintaining them.

On Tuesday, August 23, 2011, a 5.8 magnitude earthquake struck just southwest of Washington D.C., which resulted in damaging the Washington Monument. 50% of the funds needed to repair the monument came as an amazingly patriotic gift from a private businessman, David Rubenstein. Congress appropriated a matching amount of money to accomplish the needed repairs. As much as Mr. Rubenstein's gift is appreciated and applauded, it is appalling to me that the Government of the United States of America would not have addressed this completely.

In the fall of 2014 inside the Jefferson Memorial, a five foot long, three foot wide chunk of limestone fell from part of the ceiling due to water damage from malfunctioning gutters. Thankfully, no one was injured. But again, due to reactive rather than proactive maintenance of our National Monuments, this was allowed to deteriorate to this unacceptable point.

These are only some of the more noticeable / newsworthy examples of the underfunded Park Service which is tasked with the maintenance of these monuments along with the vast areas of National Parks nationally. Our short sighted, irresponsible budgeting wherein we are not taking proper care of our infrastructure ends up costing more, eventually, as anyone who has ever owned a house, or a boat, would well understand.

We are smarter than this. We know better than to do this. We should investigate and identify exactly what and how much to budget to properly maintain our National Parks, memorials, bridges, roads and just do it.

Chapter 5. NAFTA / WTO / MFN Rescinded

Tariffs allow a nation to tax imports, which raises the price on imported goods, letting more expensive locally-produced goods compete with cheaper imports. Without that protection, products that are more efficiently or cheaply produced in another nation will likely no longer be produced locally as cheaper imports are allowed to enter the market. This creates job displacement or unemployment in each nation, which may or may not be balanced out by the expanding of other industries.

An agreement between the United States and some of our nearest trading partners, called the North American Free Trade Agreement or NAFTA, went into effect on January 1, 1994.

The Effects of NAFTA
From http://www.inc.com/encyclopedia/north-american-free-trade-agreement-nafta.html

"Since NAFTA's passage, American business interests have often expressed great satisfaction with the agreement. Trade has grown sharply between the three nations who are parties to NAFTA but that increase of trade activity has resulted in rising trade deficits for the U.S. with both Canada and Mexico—the U.S. imports more from Mexico and Canada than it exports to these trading partners. Critics of the agreement argue that NAFTA has been at least partially responsible for these trade deficits as well as the **striking loss of manufacturing jobs experienced in the U.S.** over the last decade."

At NAFTA's 20th anniversary, *Public Citizen* published a report that details the results.

"… *a staggering $181 billion U.S. trade deficit with NAFTA partners: Mexico and Canada and the loss of 1 million net U.S. jobs under NAFTA, growing income inequality, displacement of more than one million Mexican farmers and a doubling of illegal immigration from Mexico.*"

The study points out that instead of the specific promises coming true made by U.S. corporations like GE, Chrysler and Caterpillar to create specific numbers of American jobs if NAFTA was approved, the government data shows that instead, they fired U.S. workers and moved operations to Mexico. The data also shows how post-NAFTA trade and investment trends have contributed to middle-class pay cuts, which in turn contributed to growing income inequality.

Another point from the study:

"*U.S. trade deficit growth with Mexico and Canada has been 45 percent higher than with countries not party to a U.S. Free Trade Agreement, and U.S. manufacturing exports to Canada and Mexico have grown at less than half the pre-NAFTA rate."*

NAFTA's tracked outcomes prove how damaging this type of agreement is for most people. The evidence makes clear that job-offshoring incentives will be utilized, with the obvious negative effects on people. As Americans have experienced NAFTA's effects, public opinion has shifted too. What was originally a narrow divide during the 1993 NAFTA debate, has turned into an overwhelming opposition today. A *2012 Angus Reid Public Opinion* poll found that:

> *".. only 15 percent believe the U.S. should "continue to be a member of NAFTA." That opposition cuts across party lines, class divisions and education levels."*

This non-partisan public opposition to NAFTA-style pacts is what underlies the growing opposition in Congress to President Obama's request that Congress delegate away its constitutional authorities through *Fast Track* trade authority. Were it not for the creation of a legislative fast track through Congress for NAFTA, the agreement would most likely not have been implemented.

Fast Track "Trade Promotion Authority" (TPA), established by the Trade Act of 1974 was a plan designed under the administration of Richard Nixon that has only been used 16 times, including for NAFTA. It empowered a president to sign a trade agreement before Congress voted on it, with the authority given to the executive branch to write legislation not subject to committee review that would implement the pact and even alter existing, related U.S. laws. Fast Track required House and Senate votes on this bill within 90 days, with all floor amendments forbidden and a maximum of 20 hours of debate.

In the 19 years since NAFTA and the agreement establishing the World Trade Organization were passed under Fast Track, Congress has realized that these pacts rewrote wide swaths of non-trade laws, and Democratic and GOP presidents have had a hard time convincing Congress to accept further Fast Track implementations.

Fast Track had only been in effect for five years (2002-2007) when the same group of businesses, i.e., agribusiness, Big Pharma, oil and gas giants and the think tanks they fund, began lobbying Congress to revive Fast Track because they knew that was the only way the Trans Pacific Partnership (TPP) could get through Congress. Political difficulties, particularly those related to the acceptance of the Trade Promotion Authority (TPA) by Congress, presents another cause of delay for the TPP negotiations. Receiving TPA from Congress is especially difficult for President Obama since members of his own Democratic Party are against them, while Republicans generally support the trade talks. Bottom line: this is stalled in Congress. Thank God.

Other NAFTA findings after 20 years of study:
- Rather than creating the net 200,000 jobs per year promised by former President Bill Clinton on the basis of the Peterson Institute for International Economics projections, job loss from NAFTA began rapidly.
- American manufacturing jobs were lost as U.S. firms used NAFTA's new foreign investor privileges to relocate production to Mexico to take advantage of that country's lower wages and weaker environmental standards. U.S. job erosion

worsened as a new flood of NAFTA imports swamped gains in exports, creating a massive new trade deficit that equated to an estimated **net loss of one million U.S. jobs by 2004**. A small pre-NAFTA U.S. trade surplus of $2.5 billion with Mexico turned into a huge new deficit, and a pre-NAFTA $29.1 billion deficit with Canada exploded. The NAFTA-spurred job loss has not abated during NAFTA's second decade, as the burgeoning post-NAFTA U.S. trade deficit with Canada and Mexico has not declined.

- More than 845,000 U.S. workers in the manufacturing sector have been certified for Trade Adjustment Assistance (TAA) since NAFTA, because they lost their jobs due to imports from Canada and Mexico or the relocation of factories to those countries. The TAA program is quite narrow, covering only a subset of jobs lost at manufacturing facilities, and is difficult to qualify for. Thus, the NAFTA TAA numbers significantly undercount NAFTA job loss.

NAFTA contributed to downward pressure on U.S. wages and growing income inequality. According to the U.S. Bureau of Labor Statistics, two out of every three displaced manufacturing workers who were rehired in 2012 experienced wage reductions, most were more than 20 percent lower. As increasing numbers of workers displaced from manufacturing jobs joined the glut of workers competing for non-offshorable, low-skill jobs in sectors such as hospitality and food service, real wages have also fallen in these sectors since NAFTA. The resulting downward pressure on wages has fueled recent growth in income inequality.

Scores of NAFTA countries' environmental and health laws have been challenged in foreign tribunals through the controversial "*investor-state*" dispute resolution system. Foreign corporations have extracted more than $360 million in compensation from NAFTA governments via investor-state tribunal challenges against toxics bans, land-use rules, water and forestry policies and more. More than $12.4 billion is currently pending in such claims, including challenges of medicine patent policies, a fracking moratorium and a renewable energy program.

The average annual U.S. agricultural trade deficit with Mexico and Canada under NAFTA stands at $800 million, more than twice the pre-NAFTA level. U.S. beef imports from Mexico and Canada, for example, have risen 130 percent since NAFTA. This stands in stark contrast to the promises made to U.S. farmers and ranchers that NAFTA would allow them to export their way to newfound wealth and farm income stability. Despite an overall 188 percent rise in food imports from Canada and Mexico under NAFTA, the average nominal price of food in the United States has jumped 65 percent since NAFTA went into effect.

The reductions in consumer goods prices that have materialized have not been sufficient to offset the losses to wages under NAFTA. U.S. workers without college degrees (63 % of the workforce) likely have lost a net amount equal to 12.2 percent of their wages under NAFTA-style trade even after accounting for gains from cheaper goods. This net loss means a loss of more than $3,300 per year for a worker earning the median annual wage of $27,500.

The export of subsidized U.S. corn did increase under NAFTA, destroying the livelihoods of more than one million Mexican *campesino* farmers and about 1.4 million additional Mexican workers whose livelihoods depended on agriculture. The desperate migration of those displaced from Mexico's rural economy pushed down wages in Mexico's border *maquiladora factory zone* and contributed to a doubling of Mexican immigration to the United States following NAFTA's implementation.

Though the price paid to Mexican farmers for corn plummeted after NAFTA, the deregulated retail price of tortillas - Mexico's staple food - shot up 279 percent in the pact's first 10 years. Facing displacement, rising prices and stagnant wages, more than half the Mexican population, and more than 60 percent of the rural population, still falls below the poverty line, despite the promises that NAFTA would bring broad prosperity to Mexicans.

Real wages in Mexico have fallen significantly below pre-NAFTA levels as price increases for basic consumer goods have exceeded wage increases. A minimum wage earner in Mexico today can buy 38 percent fewer consumer goods than on the day that NAFTA took effect. Despite promises that NAFTA would benefit Mexican consumers by granting access to cheaper imported products, the cost of basic consumer goods in Mexico has risen to seven times the pre-NAFTA level, while the minimum wage stands at only four times the pre-NAFTA level.

Despite the overwhelming evidence of NAFTA's failure, the Obama administration has made it a priority to sign the TPP, a sweeping pact with 11 Pacific Rim nations premised on expanding the NAFTA model. Past efforts to expand

NAFTA throughout Latin America via a Free Trade Area of the Americas and to Asia via an Asia-Pacific Economic Cooperation (APEC) Free Trade Agreement failed as the major economies in each region sought to avoid the damage they observed NAFTA causing within the United States and Mexico.

Given NAFTA's devastating outcomes, few of the corporations or think tanks that sold it as a boon for all of us in the 1990s like to talk about it, but the reality is that their promises failed as millions of people were severely harmed. Now, the same interests that promoted NAFTA to the public are at it again to push the TPP, but the difference is that 20 years of the NAFTA experience has turned Americans against these sorts of deals. As President, I would do all that I could to rescind the NAFTA agreement, ASAP.

The Chinese Middle Class

The next section is about how we created the Chinese Middle Class, at the cost of our own. I couldn't introduce this any better than *Bloomberg View* did, so I am presenting the beginning of their article, "Guess What's Destroying the Middle Class?," by Noah Smith (contributor to *Bloomberg View*

- *http://www.bloombergview.com/articles/2015-03-25/what-s-in-store-for-america-s-workforce*) :

> *"Perhaps the biggest question in American political economy right now is why middle-class wages have been falling. There are three main hypotheses. Roughly, these are: Robots, unions and China. The robots theory gets by far the most play in the news media, since it's by far the scariest -- if automation is replacing big chunks of the human workforce, things are only going to get worse as robots become more capable and efficient. This interpretation has tentatively been embraced by many on the political right, since*

it doesn't imply a need for substantial government intervention in the economy (though it might imply a need for redistribution). The unions theory is favored by the political left, since it implies that giving more institutional power to this traditional liberal power bloc would shift the distribution of national income toward workers.

Neither side really wants to blame China. The right generally represents business interests and capital owners who have made a lot of money off of China, and hope to make a lot more. The left is afraid to go against the free-trade orthodoxy that has dominated postwar American economic thinking, and also fears a potential cold war with China.

But there's just one problem: The evidence may point to the least favored answer being the right one."

After quoting the various studies by globally recognized economists who describe in great detail that as the imports from China have increased, the American Middle Class has been negatively impacted, the article states:

"Rising imports cause higher unemployment, lower labor force participation, and reduced wages in local labor markets that house import competing manufacturing industries.. ...import competition explains one-quarter of the contemporaneous aggregate decline in US manufacturing employment.

In other words, there is a growing body of research showing that globalization -- and, in particular, the rise of China -- has been the biggest factor hollowing out the American middle class."

Then the article comes to the most important question: *What can we do about this?* Here is this article's answer:

"The only solution to the problem of globalization may be to wait. Chinese wages have risen a lot, and only India is big enough to

take China's place. As global economic convergence proceeds, the U.S. will look more attractive as an investment destination, and reshoring will increase. That isn't an answer that people want to hear, but it may be the right one."

Rather than wait for the American Middle Class to stagnate long enough and deep enough to equal the rising Third World or Developing Countries, I would select to at least stop the bleeding by rescinding our participation in NAFTA, the WTO, and removing the *"most favored nation"* Trading Status from China. Since 1998, the term Normal Trade Relations (NTR) has replaced *most favored nation* in all U.S. statutes. In China's case, Congress agreed to *permanent normal trade relations* (PNTR) status in Public Law (P.L.) 106-286, which President Clinton signed into law on October 10, 2000. This will also be rescinded, ASAP.

The most vocal entities who will complain, besides China, will be the Agricultural interests who opposed attempts to block MFN / NTR renewal for China, after the massacre of pro-democracy demonstrators in Tiananmen Square, contending that several billion dollars annually in current and future U.S. agricultural exports could be jeopardized if that country retaliated. I'm not worried that there won't be other markets for food; I'm worried about the American Middle Class and would therefore easily make that decision.

In summation, considering the well documented negative effects to our Middle Class, jobs, and lifestyle, with volumes of deeply negative societal ramifications, I would remove our participation in NAFTA, the WTO, and sever all MFN / NTR designations specifically with China. However, I wouldn't provide this return to protectionism without strings. Given new life without the overwhelming flood of cheap imports, our manufacturing enterprises must come back, not just as good as the Chinese, but better.

'*Made in America*' must mean it is the best in the world, so I will be personally visiting the resurging American factories and companies manufacturing products as diverse as cell phones, TVs / monitors, microwaves, washers and dryers to computers and even clothes. These visits will be to personally inspire greater efforts and design improvements.

As a nation we must utilize the chance these trade changes will provide to rebuild, redesign and regroup better than ever before. I will therefore strongly support Governmental assistance—grants, loans, whatever it takes—to provide the resources for the American Companies to have the time to rebuild themselves better than they could otherwise.

Our Government enacted flawed laws which hurt many people for an entire generation, the least we can do is proactively help repair the damage. From their factory designs to their product designs, with environmental considerations strongly considered, we can rebuild the manufacturing enterprises in America, so well that the world will want our products not because of pricing, which we can't compete on with developing nations, but because they are so clearly the best available, last the longest, and provide the greatest amount of quality features.

We must rebrand *American Made* into the *Best in the World*. And with the combination of the US Government and US entrepreneurial / business minds, we can do this better than anyone else.

Chapter 6. End the H1B Program

After reading this chapter's title, you are quite possibly wondering: what is the 'H1B Program'? I will allow the United States Department of Labor, Wage and Hour Division to provide their definition:

"The H-1B program applies to employers seeking to hire nonimmigrant aliens as workers in specialty occupations or as fashion models of distinguished merit and ability. A specialty occupation is one that requires the application of a body of highly specialized knowledge and the attainment of at least a bachelor's degree or its equivalent. The intent of the H-1B provisions is to help employers who cannot otherwise obtain needed business skills and abilities from the U.S. workforce by authorizing the temporary employment of qualified individuals who are not otherwise authorized to work in the United States.

The law establishes certain standards in order to protect similarly employed U.S. workers from being adversely affected by the employment of the nonimmigrant workers, as well as to protect the H-1B nonimmigrant workers. Employers must attest to the Department of Labor that they will pay wages to the H-1B nonimmigrant workers that are at least equal to the actual wage paid by the employer to other workers with similar experience and qualifications for the job in question, or the prevailing wage for the occupation in the area of intended employment – whichever is greater.

The number of new visas that can be issued each year is subject to a cap. H-1B visas are capped at 65,000 during a fiscal year; an additional 20,000 are available to those individuals who received a master's degree or higher from a U.S. institution of higher education. H-1B1 visas are limited to 1,400 nationals of Chile and 5,400 nationals of Singapore; E-3 visas are limited to 10,500 nationals of Australia.

Additional rules apply to employers who are dependent upon H-1B workers or are willful violators of the H-1B rules. An H-1B dependent employer is, generally, one whose H-1B workers comprise 15 percent or more of the employer's total workforce. Different thresholds apply to smaller employers. H-1B dependent employers who wish to hire only H-1B workers who are paid at least $60,000 per year or have a master's degree or higher in a specialty related to the employment, can be exempted from these additional rules.

H-1B dependent employers and willful violator employers must attest to the following three elements addressing non-displacement and recruitment of U.S. workers:

The employer will not displace any similarly employed U.S. worker within 90 days before or after applying for H-1B status, or an extension of status for any H-1B worker;

The employer will not place any H-1B worker employed pursuant to the LCA at the worksite of another employer unless the employer first makes a bona fide inquiry as to whether the other employer has displaced or intends to displace a similarly employed U.S. worker within 90 days before or after the placement of the H-1B worker; and

The employer, before applying for H-1B status for any alien worker pursuant to an H-1B LCA, took good faith steps to recruit U.S. workers for the job for which the alien worker is sought, at wages at least equal to those offered to the H-1B worker. Also, the employer will offer the job to any U.S. worker who applies and is equally or better qualified than the H-1B worker. This attestation does not apply if the H-1B worker is a "priority worker" (see Section 203(b) (1) (A), (B), or (C) of the INA)."

Okay... Got all of that? Well, please allow me to summarize.

American employers can utilize foreign workers when they can't find an American to fulfill the job opening. There are annual caps in the tens of thousands, for new applications for H1B employees, and an existing H1B employee is allowed into the United States for an initial period of three years—extendable to six years and ten if unique conditions exist.

There are hundreds of thousands of H1B foreign employees currently working inside America, (In 2012, 262,569 new visas were approved with 136,890 being for initial employment and 125,679 being for continued employment), primarily in professional trades, such as computer programmers. According to the rules / laws within the H1B Program, these H1B employees can't be paid less than the *'prevailing wage'*:

"The employer pays H-1B non-immigrants the same wage level paid to all other individuals with similar experience and qualifications for that specific employment, or the prevailing wage for the occupation in the area of employment, whichever is higher."

Now that the stage is set, we can explore what is really happening. Before proceeding, I should share that I have been a computer consultant for decades. During this time, I have provided my services to a generally well known list of clients from California to Boston to Southern Florida to Indianapolis. Until roughly the year 2000, like most people in my career niche, I experienced nothing but annual rate increases (raises) in my hourly rate, which was also accelerated each time I changed contracts, i.e., provided my services to a new client.

Around the year 2000, the rate I could charge for my services plateaued. Along with that, the demand for my services, which had been so much in demand that I could get a new contract before lunch, now required at least 3-4 months, sometimes longer, to obtain a new contract.

What happened? The relentless influx of H1B computer programmers diluted the rate which I, and my fellow American colleagues could charge, due to the H1Bs' lower rates. Only because of my decades of experience, coupled with my excellent references, was I able to maintain the plateaued rate, which was still appreciably higher than the H1Bs' rates. Now I have to find clients who value my level of expertise enough to pay above what has become the common rate in the United States, which clearly reduces the number of opportunities open to me. Thus, the 3 - 4 months in between contracts.

Realizing a change had occurred in my career, I researched the situation and learned that in Great Britain, which does not have H1Bs, i.e., *discount technical workers*, the rate for my specific skill set had continued to rise, which had gone from less than Americans were paid to roughly 30 – 40% more. And is still rising. But not in America.

I have also experienced, first hand, numerous client sites which have terminated their American programmers and replaced them with H1Bs, *in direct conflict with the laws* as posted earlier in this chapter. Granted, these companies generally provide their terminated employees with generous termination packages, following tiered payment schedules based on how many years they served their employer. How nice of them.

Most recently, I was specifically contracted by a company called Cognizant, (who provided the H1Bs to their client: Covidien, in Mansfield Mass.), to facilitate the 'knowledge transfer' sessions from the soon to be terminated American programmers to the *replacement* onsite H1B and offshore programmers.

I had not been told this would be my specific task during this contract until my first day on site. During my previous interviews for the job, they had only told me that I would be in charge of the 'AS/400 Tower' which was their designation of one of their development groups.

During these *knowledge transfer sessions*, the Americans were extremely uncomfortable dealing with their replacements, as well you might expect, and they clearly saw me as a traitor— an American helping foreign replacements. As the sessions continued, more than once, one or another of the Americans broke down from their extreme emotional upheaval. This was unbelievably difficult to witness and to be a part of.

I was extremely vocal with my Cognizant supervisor about

the unacceptability of this entire operation which led to my early termination from the contract. From my perspective, I was greatly relieved to be out of this obscenity even though it took me roughly 5 months to find another contract. During that time, I worked as a host at a local restaurant and earned a fraction of my usual income. Nevertheless, as you may confirm with my wife, I was a much happier person being unconnected to such a heinous action.

This is going on all over America. And not just to computer programmers. Engineers, registered nurses, a lot of good paying, technically skilled American jobs are being filled by these discount third world people. Many companies act as the agents providing the H1Bs to the American client companies and they are reaping huge profits.

Ranking	H1B Sponsor	# of H1B Applicants
1	INFOSYS Limited	23,759
2	TATA Consultancy Services Limited	14,098
3	WIPRO Limited	8,365
4	DeLoitte Consulting LLP	7,017
5	Accenture LLP	5,498
6	IBM India Private Limited	5,029
7	HCL America, Inc.	4,749
8	Larsen & Toubro InfoTech Limited	3,939
9	Microsoft Corporation	3,750
10	Ernst & Young U.S. LLP	3,727

Figure 15 - Top 10 H1B Sponsors for 2014

You might wonder how so many thousands of people are illegally being provided for LESS than the prevailing wage to the American employers, in conflict with the law that states they should be paid at least the same amount. During my experience with this business, I have learned how this is accomplished.

First, our Congress has not provided enough funding to the Federal Department of Employment to accomplish enforcement of the H1B laws and regulations. Their budget barely covers the annual *rubber stamping* of the H1B applications let alone providing the resources to confirm that these workers are at the locations declared on their applications.

The H1B sponsor company will declare to the INS that H1B worker X will be at a specific address, which might very well be an office for the H1B sponsor company. Since all of their H1Bs are also declared as working at this address, it is true that this new H1B applicant will be paid the same prevailing wage as the other employees *at that address*. However, what is not declared is that the H1B will actually be working at: Microsoft, GE, Sylvania, Staples, LL Bean, or _____ fill in the blank. Many hundreds if not thousands of employers around the nation are utilizing these discount workers.

In direct conflict with the H1B law, the H1Bs' rate of pay is not being compared to American employees at their actual work place. Without an adequate number of personnel at the local branches of the Federal Employment Department to do any follow up/checking, this method of skirting the law works. And it's not just the Americans who are suffering. The vast majority of H1B placements are paid appreciably lower rates than the Americans who provide similar services. Once inside the United States, the H1B consultant can't switch jobs from their 'sponsor' employer. They must accept and fulfill their contract or leave the country. This is called exploitation.

Obviously, American companies would not replace their American employees with H1B people unless they save money, which proves that the H1B rules and laws are not being adhered to. This also explains the vast amount of lobbying from these companies in the halls of Congress to increase the annual H1B quotas. This constant drum beat of lobbyists requesting annual increases of the H1B quotas is declared to be on the basis of *not being able to find Americans* to fill the demand for these skills. This is only true if you include the reality that what they are actually looking for, are people who will do these jobs for less than Americans charge.

It should also be noted that my competitors for the Presidency are all voicing their support of increasing the H1B quotas. Most people are unaware of how underhanded and un-American this action is, and how many people are being severely affected by this program. Much of the public believes this is good for America, because, as they are told, this will *keep us competitive with the world.* Amazingly, even though there have been hundreds, if not thousands of claims and complaints and articles and news stories about the injustice of the Americans' displacement to make room for the H1Bs, rarely is anything done. Meanwhile, the quotas are increased every few years. *Money talks,* comes to mind.

Congress and the majority of Federal Employment Department administrators know very well exactly what is going on, yet, considering the lack of enough money being budgeted for enforcement; Congress has designed this activity to successfully continue undetected and unabated. In the meantime, Federal Employment Department people can't do anything about it except continue to rubber stamp the

H1B applications.

Besides the illegal displacement of Americans from high paying professions, there is another associated negative ramification to the abuse of the H1B Program. By providing negative / downward pressures on both demand and pay rates for IT and other career professionals, students who are deciding which career path to follow will be dissuaded from these H1B diluted professions if they research the pay rates. This increases the validity and supports the vicious cycle of not having enough Americans to fulfill American high tech jobs. We as a nation are being lulled into leaving these jobs to the foreigners who are willing to do them. This is a very unhealthy direction for our country to take.

I want to see Americans doing as much as possible ourselves, for ourselves and for the world, rather than depending upon others to do the work for us. We want to be a healthy self-sustaining society, with more and more opportunities for Americans to succeed at and grow with. As President, it would be my great pleasure to terminate the H1B program, ASAP.

Once this abused program is terminated and the H1Bs are sent home, I envision a great increase in the demand for replacements for the hundreds of thousands of the now vacant IT and other skilled jobs. The pay rates for these skill sets would rise and the next wave of students looking for careers will be greatly inspired to enter those specialty areas. This will definitely benefit Americans and America as a whole. The Corporate sponsors of the H1B lobbyists will have to sell better and/or more products to increase their profits rather than use foreign discount workers to displace Americans.

Chapter 7. All Foreign Alliances Reviewed per American Principles

As the President, I would have the primary responsibility of representing the United States of America to the world. Under the Constitution, the president is the federal official that is primarily responsible for the relations of the United States with foreign nations. Okay, so what would I do in this area?

First of all, I would re-think who we are supporting and who we are not. I do not believe we should be supporting any government or monarchy which does not properly deal with their own citizens, per our own basic principles of Justice for ALL and equality under the law. Our Principles and Laws are what we have fought for, too many times, to forget all about them whenever we go 200 miles off our own coasts.

As a Bostonian, wherever I go, I am still a Red Sox fan. It doesn't matter if I am in California, Florida or Indianapolis; I am still a Red Sox fan. That is part of what makes me who I am. Sorry Yankee fans, but this rivalry is one of the wonderful pleasures of baseball in America, so I suggest we enjoy it rather than me trying to hide it to be politically correct. In that same mindset, I am an American. And as such, wherever I go, I am still an American who believes and follows and respects the American Principles and Laws which are based upon basic human decency, right vs. wrong, and Justice for ALL. If country X, Y, or Z doesn't follow these basic principles then I am not going to support them in their oppression, inhumanity, exploitation, or any other injustices of their people. What kind of an American would I be if I did support them for their oil, or their influence, or their trade, or whatever? We are better than that. We do not need anyone's oil, or trade, or influence, or whatever so much that we should forget that America is the home of Justice for ALL.

During the Cold War, we saw alliances as a method of offsetting the Soviets in a global strategy. Well, the Soviets are gone. And we are the only Super Power on Earth. So, what is our excuse for forgetting our Principles now? If a Saudi Arabian citizen is overheard saying something negative about their monarch, and a member of the Royal Family hears about this indiscretion, it is quite possible that person will be dragged out of their bed in the middle of the night, never to be heard from again. Yet, the United States of America is training and selling arms to the House of Saud and their Royal Guard to maintain control over their people. As a result, the House of Saud likes us a lot, but the millions of Saudi Arabians sure don't.

We are supporting their oppressors with arms and training and political support too.

This must stop. If they won't sell us any oil because we

won't give or sell them any arms, so be it. We'll use our own oil, or buy it from someone else. However, my belief is that if we wanted to buy their oil, they would still sell it to us. Even if we stuck to our own principles and refused to support their oppression of their own people. By doing this, the PEOPLE of Saudi Arabia would know and respect America for truly being the Home of Justice for ALL, unlike what we are to them today. I would much rather not be the enemy of millions of people in order to be the friends of an oppressive regime.

While Mubarak was the President of Egypt, for decades, we supported him and his regime. It required a revolution by the people of Egypt to oust him, which we witnessed as an early part of the 'Arab Spring'.

Why had the United States of America supported Mubarak instead of the people of Egypt? How could we provide our support of military hardware, money, and political support to the unacceptable authoritarian regime of Mubarak knowing full well that the people were being suppressed from their rightful freedoms?

As President of the United States, I would not support a 'Mubarak' type regime with anything beyond a copy of our Bill of Rights, and Constitution as an advisement of how to properly treat people.

Then, there is the little country of Israel. A country created in the late 1940s by an invasion of partially armed and trained terrorists from Europe after WWII, the Lehi, the Irgun, the Stern Gang, and others who bombed, burned, robbed, assassinated and massacred people until the British had enough and abandoned the area. After the Massacre of Deir Yassein, a relatively small village on a strategically important road for the invaders, the civilians ran for their lives in a mass exodus and became refugees, which they still are to this day. Soon after this exodus, the perpetrators of this terrorist campaign upon civilians were recognized as a sovereign State, and went overnight from being *invading terrorists* to the country of Israel.

The United Nations advised the new country of Israel to either pay the refugees for what was confiscated or allow them to return to their homes. Israel refused to do this, and has steadfastly refused to resolve the plight and the epic injustice which they perpetrated upon their victims the Palestinians. This has inspired decades of a never ending vicious cycle of hatred and violence between the Refugees and their occupying oppressors.

Initially, America was not too excited about supporting Israel, however as time went on, as an offset to the Soviet alliances with the Arab countries, we saw a value in expanding our relationship with Israel, until today, our Vice President says repeatedly: *"there can be no light between us."* By supporting Israel even as she continues to steal more land via settlements and maintains an inhumane oppression, occupation, and even a blockade of people in an area of land called Gaza, these victims are associating America with their hated oppressors, and consider us much more their enemy than their friend.

America can't support this anymore. In fact, it might well be that because of our over the top support of the Israelis, they have been able to arrogantly stick to a 'might is right' policy and not seek a peaceful resolution with their victims the Palestinian refugees.

I firmly believe that if we return to our Principles, with all our foreign relations and policies, with all nations of the world, the PEOPLE of the world will respect and admire us instead of hating and despising us, and will no longer plan and scheme of ways to hurt us. Therefore, we will support the oppressed, not their oppressors, whoever those might be. Granted, some governments and regimes and questionable entities might not like us anymore, but they are vastly outnumbered by the people of the world, who I am sure we are supposed to be humane and fair with, even if they are outside of our borders.

America will be the 'good guys' again, so help me God.

This new policy of foreign relations is the only way to actually end the *War on Terrorism* peacefully, and forever. An outcome that every American would greatly appreciate happening sooner rather than never. Playing Whack-a-Mole in the Middle East is opening ourselves up to what one person claimed was the way to defeat us – *Death by a thousand cuts.* We must stop being so arrogant as to think we can do this endlessly. We can't. Nobody can, or should.

Our greatest 'strength' is not derived from bullets, as much as many would crudely support that concept. It is from our American Principles: Justice for ALL, and Equality under the Law. We must never forget that, and never sell those principles out for political, financial, or any supposed 'gains' whatsoever, not ever again. That is what sets America apart from the other countries of the world, not our bullets.

I am not a pacifist, I am an American. We don't have to kill people to exist, to grow, or to be happy. Our basis is mutual respect and individual rights, and a day's pay for a day's work, which means we believe and depend upon Justice for ALL. Not bullets. We will maintain our position of strength by maintaining our principles, our freedoms, and our rights. That, and having the most advanced military in the world, will work together to keep the forces of evil aimed elsewhere. Given our rights and freedoms, Americans are—individually and as a group—stronger than anyone. Nobody can defeat that. Nobody.

I stand up as a candidate for President who would not deploy any machines of war except to defend the United States from a direct attack of us or our right to peace and justice globally. And, if I would order such an action, I would be at the front. I couldn't order the men and women of our Armed Forces into harm's way while I sit back in Washington. I would take the title: *Commander in Chief* very literally.

Okay, time to change the subject.

Still within the subject of foreign policies, another conflict with common sense comes to mind. *How can we give billions of dollars away to other countries while we are concurrently borrowing billions, and even trillions of dollars?*

I can't imagine explaining to my wife that we should take cash out of our credit card accounts and give it away on the street. As much as she loves and supports me, I am absolutely sure she would not agree to that insanity. But, that is exactly what we are doing as a nation.

In fiscal year 2012, the U.S. government allocated the

following amounts for aid:

Total economic and military assistance: $48.4 billion

Total military assistance: $17.2 billion

Total economic assistance: $31.2 billion

Figure 16 displays what we owe as a rolling debt from 2000 to 2014.

Date	Dollar Amount
09/30/2014	17,824,071,380,733.82
09/30/2013	16,738,183,526,697.32
09/30/2012	16,066,241,407,385.89
09/30/2011	14,790,340,328,557.15
09/30/2010	13,561,623,030,891.79
09/30/2009	11,909,829,003,511.75
09/30/2008	10,024,724,896,912.49
09/30/2007	9,007,653,372,262.48
09/30/2006	8,506,973,899,215.23
09/30/2005	7,932,709,661,723.50
09/30/2004	7,379,052,696,330.32
09/30/2003	6,783,231,062,743.62
09/30/2002	6,228,235,965,597.16
09/30/2001	5,807,463,412,200.06
09/30/2000	5,674,178,209,886.86

Figure 16 – U.S. Rolling Debt, 2000 to 2014

This chart shows our debt is rising by just less than $1 trillion per year, while we are giving away almost $50 billion. $50 billion is only roughly 5% of how much our debt is rising annually, but if we are ever going to pay off our debt and get our financial house in balance, we have to stop giving away money while we are still borrowing it.

I understand that a good amount of the military aid we provide comes with the stipulation that they must use their grant money to buy American arms, however, this still isn't a healthy path. We are, in effect, pushing military weapons onto countries which wouldn't be able to afford them if we didn't give them these weapons. Wouldn't it be a lot safer for humanity if we allowed the international levels of weaponry to naturally seek its own level? The more we arm countries, the more people end up being killed. This is not a wonderful situation for America to be supporting even if Lockheed earns a few billion dollars more from it.

We are printing and borrowing money, in order to indirectly subsidize our own weapons manufacturers and distributing these powerful weapons for free, to many nations. WOW. On so many levels this is just plain wrong. As President, I would end foreign military aid first, then drastically reduce other foreign aid, too. The only exceptions would be for those critically important humanitarian efforts, which should be supported while creating an international humanitarian fund that would eventually remove the burden from us. A consortium of nations could more efficiently handle these efforts then us alone.

While this might seem to be an embarrassment for the United States, in reality it's exhibiting fiscal sanity. This is undeniable in the face of our national debt approaching critical mass. Along with the tax code changes, re-instated tariffs and other changes I would support, we must be fiscally responsible with ourselves and to the world if we are to be able to maintain ourselves into the future. We surely do not want to be a house built on debt, which would easily collapse if anything goes wrong.

I will be a responsible President and make cuts where ever possible to restore our balance sheet to the positive. Once there, we can re-explore with whom and how we might be benefactors again. We can be much more helpful globally in the long run if we don't destroy ourselves from simple fiscal irresponsibility. This is just common sense.

Chapter 8. Global Focus: Environmental Responsibility

As a sailing enthusiast, I have a personal connection with the oceans. That connection is further defined by a deep respect for their beauty, their importance to our lives and their raw power. A few years ago when I first heard about the huge mass of plastic debris being carried around a large area in the Pacific Ocean by the currents, it turned my stomach that mankind would allow this to remain out there. This isn't just an inconsequential or unimportant issue, even from the hardest most pragmatic person's point of view. This plastic is breaking down into smaller and smaller particles and being consumed by a wide array of marine life. Some of these indigestible plastics end up in the stomachs of fish, marine birds and animals, and their young. Included among the many species of wildlife affected are sea turtles and the Black-footed Albatross,.

The Midway Atoll receives substantial amounts of debris from this floating plastic patch. Of the 1.5 million Laysan Albatrosses that inhabit Midway, when examined, nearly all are found to have plastic in their digestive system.

Approximately one-third of their chicks die each year, and many of those deaths are due to their parents feeding them plastic. Twenty tons of plastic debris washes up on Midway every year with five tons of that debris fed to Albatross chicks.

The remains of dead baby albatrosses reveal the far-reaches of plastic pollution on Midway Atoll, 2000 miles from any mainland. Credit: Chris Jordan, from his series "Midway: Message from the Gyre." Used under Creative Commons Attribution-Noncommercial-No Derivative Works 3.0 United States License.

Figure 17 – Remains of Dead Baby Albatrosses due to Plastic Consumption

Besides these particles' danger to wildlife, on the microscopic level the floating debris can absorb organic pollutants from seawater, including PCBs, DDT, and PAHs, all known carcinogens. Aside from toxic effects, when ingested some of these are mistaken by the endocrine system as *estradiol*, causing hormone disruption in the affected animal. These toxin-containing plastic pieces are also eaten by jellyfish, which are then eaten by larger fish. Many of these fish are then consumed by humans, resulting in their ingestion of all of these toxic chemicals.

This is incredibly bad for everyone!

Figure 18 depicts a graphic display of the areas in the Pacific where this plastic pollution is swirling around.

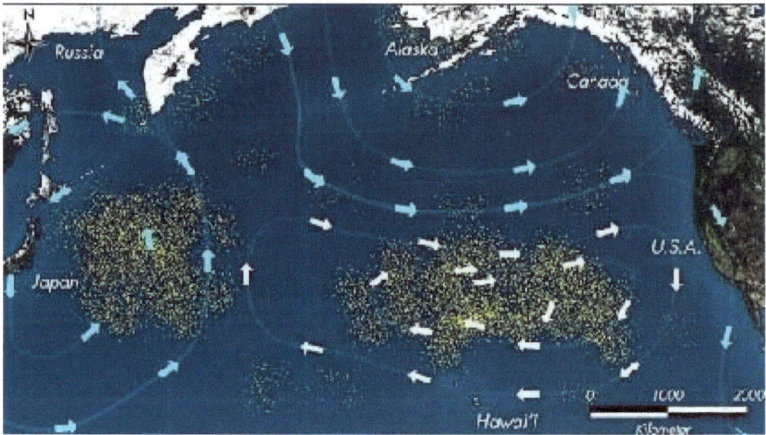

Figure 18 - Floating Plastic Pollution in the Pacific

Plastic doesn't biodegrade; even 'biodegradable' plastic just ends up breaking down into smaller and smaller pieces. These plastic particles now greatly outnumber plankton found in the area and causes massive damage to sea life when they eat it. And then we eat them. In addition to the microscopic pieces of plastic, the water is also filled with shopping bags, old flip flops, soda bottles and discarded fishing equipment.

We have to address this issue as soon as possible. And this is not just an American issue, this is a global one. *But how do you clean up something on that scale?*

"Project Kaisei (from 海星, kaisei, "ocean planet" in Japanese) is a scientific and commercial mission to study and clean up the Great Pacific Garbage Patch. The project aims to study the extent and nature of the debris with a view to capturing, detoxifying, and recycling the material, and is organized by the Ocean Voyages Institute, a California-based 501c3 non-profit organization dealing with marine preservation. The project is based in San Francisco and Hong Kong.

The project was launched on 19 March 2009, with plans for an initial phase of scientific study of the plastic debris in the North Pacific Gyre and feasibility study of the recovery and recycling technologies. The goal is to bring about a global collaboration of science, technology and solutions, to help remove some of the floating waste.

New catch methods for the debris are being studied, which would have low energy input and low marine life loss. Technologies for remediation or recycling are being evaluated, to potentially create secondary products from the waste, which in turn could help subsidize a larger scale cleanup.

The project has completed two expeditions, one in the summer of 2009, and one in 2010. New data on the issue has been collected, and more research and planning needs to be done in order to understand the metrics and costs associated with a larger scale cleanup effort.

Planning is now taking place for future research and expeditions to take place which would allow for the testing of new capture technologies and equipment, as well as the demonstration of some of the remediation or recycling technologies that could be used."

I would work with this group to coordinate their efforts

within a new United Nations administered program which would collect funds from nations using a fair algorithm to associate each country's responsibility for this plastic debris. I would also direct that some of our 'mothballed navy vessels' be re-commissioned as our contribution to this program, to be used to collect the debris.

I would further strongly suggest that the United Nations utilizes residents of the poorest of African nations or other equally needy people to be the soldiers of this clean-up effort. These people would earn a fair wage while saving the world from itself. If that isn't a 'win / win' scenario, I don't know what is.

Described within the *Project Kaisei* goals is the interest in recycling the collected debris for resale which could alleviate some of the costs of this program. I would also support an American effort in the research and development of the associated technologies to enable this recycling to succeed.

I believe we need to address this because we are capable of marshalling the various resources and expertise to accomplish it, and because we are responsible for an appreciable amount of this debris. More importantly, we are human beings and our general health will be negatively impacted by the implications of this debris upon the food supply we enjoy from the Pacific Ocean.

Chapter 9. Global Focus: The Unacceptable Abuse of Women

I have a terrible admission to make. I thought I was done writing this book and then I happened to read numerous stories about the various forms of crimes of abuse upon women. And then it struck me that I hadn't thought about this as an issue to focus on. My focus had been on taxes, trade, medical insurance, education, foreign policy, H1Bs, legalizing drugs, rebuilding bridges and roads, and even saving a black footed Albatross, but not abuse of women. I am so sorry. I stopped the editing, formatting and printing, and added this chapter; easily the most important one.

What in God's name is going on between men and women?

The same men that are stoning, burning, beating, raping, exploiting and generally abusing women in any of a thousand ways, had mothers who, with few exceptions, unconditionally loved them, fed them, clothed them, taught them, were proud of them, washed their dirty fingers and faces, wiped their asses, and did all the other things which only a mother would do for their child. Yet all of that seems to be too easily forgotten as these boys turn into men.

This is not just an American issue; this one is global. But before trying to deal with the rest of the world, as President I would deal with it domestically. Addressing the problem in the U.S. could begin with expanded punishment. That is, any violent abuse of a woman should be designated a 'Hate Crime'. This would automatically double the current sentence. This would not only discourage some 'would be' abuser(s), it would also take them out of the woman's life for a longer term. The increase in punishment should be followed by a national dialogue on how particularly heinous these crimes are, not just because women are theoretically physically weaker than men, but also because women are the *soul of our society.*

If we can allow the better side of our society to be abused with only the same reaction(s) as when these things happen to men, we aren't appropriately recognizing how very much women contribute to all of us. This is undeniably the truth. Women hold the families together. They keep us cleaner than we would be otherwise. They push us to accomplish more. They do more themselves. We've all heard the term "Super Mom." There's a reason this term has become universally used and understood. Many of them are just that. Sure, many men also push themselves and accomplish a lot, but a lot of why they do it is because of the woman in their lives.

Rather than always talking about the Sino-American dynamic, and/or the direction of the European Union, and/or the economy, or even the election(s) on those Sunday Morning Talk shows, as a 'popular President' I will make this a topic to discuss when I sit down with someone who wants to interview me. We need to discuss this with social engineers, psychiatrists, sociologists, family counselors, priests, rabbis, Imams, and try to figure out *why*; why is this happening so much, so often, so universally? Why do so many men switch from boys who respect and love their mothers into absolute and complete examples of evil trash? I can't even call them *animals* because animals wouldn't do this.

Why is the debasement and diminishment of women prevalent in so many religions? Is that where this criminal mindset starts? If we won't see women as equal to a Priest or a Rabbi are they therefore less important?

As a President, I believe I can form a blue ribbon panel to hold interviews, take testimony, do research, hire experts, all with the goal of identifying why this is happening, and what we can do to reduce the occurrences of these crimes. Then, take this on a road show, globally. Not just me, but ambassadors, and teachers, and our celebrities should join in, too. We have to make this the right thing to do, for everyone, everywhere. Hopefully, I can be a popular enough President to draw people to this issue, rather than fight me on this. Fight me on exactly what percentage of Federal Sales Tax to charge, or specifically what would be the Exemptions, but not on defending women from abuse.

Besides the actions I've outlined, I'm not sure what else can be done at this point. But, we have to start somewhere, and those are the ways I would do that. I hope we make a difference, because women are our soul and we need to treat our souls a lot better.

Chapter 10.   Summation – Vote for Me

Assuming you didn't skip all the prior content within this book, you've read the ideas I'm presenting to America in order to introduce myself and then ask for your votes. I can only hope those ideas resonated with you, as they do with me, as something to work toward. They are real ideas, with plenty of meat on those bones to really work. If we start with the ideas then do the necessary research and the work, we can accomplish what is best for the country, not just the special interest groups. Once accomplished, we can all enjoy the benefits.

When Kennedy challenged us to reach for the Moon, we didn't quibble about what this meant per any Party Agendas, we simply rolled up our sleeves, pooled our resources, worked together and within one decade, landed in the Sea of Tranquility. For those who remember that success, it should remind us how much we can do when we focus on a mutual goal. We can do anything. The proof of that dynamic is still planted on the Moon; the American Flag.

For many years now, all the candidates I have listened to have only provided high level, useless, nebulous rhetoric, without any detailed ideas to accomplish any viable goals.

Then, when one of these career politicians manages to squeak into office by hanging chads or because of the negative feelings toward a vice presidential candidate, or because of some other equally unimportant celebrity test, more by default than by positive choice, we find that we have earned another term of reactive, disappointing years, without real leadership and without any specific ideas for us to rally around and accomplish.

During President Obama's Administration, like all the other contemporary ones, we've watched the Congress and the Executive branches do their best to diminish each other, and work toward their most important goal, their next election(s), with the endless volley of 10 second sound bites with one group or another declaring how deeply they are offended, while the polls are taken, again and again. Leadership by polls is not leadership. What a waste.

Today's career politicians, without providing leadership with serious clear common sense ideas for improving our economy or tax system or foreign policies, have repeatedly turned to the tactic which works most consistently: *fear*. Most recently, since 9/11, sadly, our electorate is willing to trade individual rights for the illusion of group safety. And the politicians are only too willing to use that fear for their own agendas.

A frightened America is a very dangerous country. Dangerous to the world and to ourselves. We need a leader who will remind us that allowing fear to direct us is much more dangerous than our enemies, and taking that path will keep us from addressing what has created these enemies in the first place. As we've all heard, you have to address the cause, not the symptoms. Which is the only real *solution*.

We must remember and apply our own Principles, as we interact with the world. Justice for ALL, if universally instituted, is much more powerful than bullets if you want to enjoy a sustainable peace among human beings. I will remind us of the power of these principles given to us by our Founding Fathers as the basis of our country. And consistently apply them as I represent America to the world. If you want to be our ally, you have to recognize that basic human rights apply to everyone. I won't support anyone or any group which doesn't support Justice for ALL. Justice will do much more than drones will, if peace is the goal. That is the only real path to the *group safety* we all want, without giving up our individual rights.

Not more bullets.

I am not a politician. Most recently I have been a computer consultant, listening to my clients and observing their business process, then designing and implementing improvements. I am also a US Coast Guard Certified Charter Boat Captain; with a beautiful sailboat named the *Triumph*. I have also been a photographer, a roofer, a dishwasher, a security guard, a host of a restaurant in Boston, I sold vacuum cleaners and steak and seafood in California, and I've worked as a baker and sold clothing and sporting goods in my uncles' store in Maine. I was honorably discharged from the US Army National Guard, and been an assistant manager of a drug store in Florida. I've worn a lot of hats and done a lot of jobs in many States in this beautiful country. As a result, I have a lot of real world experience from which I would be making my decisions. I am very happily married to my beautiful wife: Evelyn and have her full and loving support.

Additionally, I am not in anyone's back pocket. Nobody has bought me or has me under their thumb. I am beholden to no one. I don't want multi-million dollar donations to my campaign. $20s and $100s would be just fine, because I won't be buying any TV ads. I want to travel around this great country and meet and talk to as many people as possible so you can see who this guy is that wants this job. Once you've talked to me, you can decide confidently.

Many of my ideas are in direct conflict with powerful forces and entities in our world. In a way, I feel as though I am volunteering once again to serve my country, and laying my life on the line for her. It was the right thing for me to do the first time, and I know it is again.

Please don't dismiss the honesty and the depth of my commitment to some personal need for celebrity or the chance to sleep in the White House. My wife and I are quite comfortable in our beautiful sailboat, while this job I am campaigning for could easily cost us all of that, and more. We aren't entering into this lightly; I am doing this to *Rebuild the United States*, ASAP. So please consider the importance of voting for me.

When Election Day arrives, please remember that the greater the margin that I win by, the stronger my mandate will be for dealing with the Congress. Please help make my job which is to accomplish what I have written in this book, easier, rather than harder. I am asking for a landslide victory! I know I will greatly enjoy having a 'real person' to vote for; I hope and trust you will too.

Thank you very much and God Bless the United States of America.

About the Author

Doug was born in Boston, MA, April 4th. His father, Albert , worked in management for TWA at Logan, and his mother, Sandra, was a housewife. Doug's early years were happy and healthy in Danvers, MA., in the North Shore area. Doug was in the second grade when his parents divorced, after which he and his mother moved around frequently. That ended when Doug entered the 8th grade and they landed in Waterville, ME, Sandra's home town. Soon after this move, Albert died of a brain tumor and left some money to Doug.

Sandra, an alcoholic by then, spent the money in bars and when that ran out, she abandoned her son in Maine in the winter of his Junior year in High School. Doug managed to complete this school year while living on the streets, then attended a Prep School in Maine called Kent's Hill for his Senior year. Doug attended a college within the University of Maine system for a short time, however without enough support, he reverted to working full time. Doug eventually returned to school in Northern California and earned a Computer Programming Certificate.

Doug has held a very wide variety of jobs throughout his life, ranging from dishwasher to computer consultant. The list includes: clothing & sporting goods store worker, (Doug's maternal family business), pizza store worker, bakery worker, roofer, photographer, photography studio and store owner, adjunct photography teacher at Colby College, door to door: vacuum cleaner salesman, steak & seafood salesman, and life insurance salesman, drug store assistant manager, security guard, US Army / National Guard member, (Honorable Discharge), mobile elementary school photographer, computer programmer which evolved into a computer consulting career providing services to client companies from California to Boston to Florida to Maine and to Indianapolis. He is also a US Coast Guard Certified Charter boat Captain wherein he and his wife Evelyn operate a sailboat chartering enterprise in Fort Lauderdale, FL., using their beautiful sailboat, the Triumph. In between computer contracts, Doug has on occasion worked as a restaurant host, in Boston, and a security guard. He does whatever it takes, as most people do.

Doug is very healthy, and he has a birth certificate from Boston. ☺

www.ingramcontent.com/pod-product-compliance
Lightning Source LLC
Chambersburg PA
CBHW040127270326
41927CB00001B/14